DREAMS OF GLORY

This is a very timely book. It touches a nerve. The issue of apocalyptic is dealt with in an immediately apparent way that links contemporary, biblical and other historical periods together in a way that displays the naturalness of apocalyptic within the human condition. 'It reads true'. The theme of hope and despair is also influential and well made and integrated into the apocalyptic spirit. I think many would not only enjoy this book but would almost find themselves awaiting its message.

Professor Douglas Davies
Department of Theology and Religions
Durham University, UK

Islam, Judaism, and Christianity are engaged not in a 'clash of civilizations' but in a sectarian conflict among branches of a single civilization traditionally steeped in apocalyptic imagery and beliefs.

Apocalypticism is a religious luxury that modern civilizations can no longer afford. Many would agree that the propagandists of the Christian Right have raised apocalyptic tensions to a dangerous level since 9/11, but in this book Richard Fenn takes on the mainline church leaders for their role in promoting an apocalyptic view of history. Those who keep apocalyptic beliefs in a respectable place in religious faith and practice must bear their share of responsibility for global terror. It is not only tragic but ironic that the churches have given apocalyptic literature such a respectable place in their sacred texts, because the apocalyptic imagination itself has its sources in non-Biblical literature: the Hellenistic prophesies that gave comfort and courage to the victims of war in the near and middle east from the time of Alexander the Great and Darius. Fenn goes on to hold apocalyptic enthusiasts in the mainline churches, as well as on the Right, responsible for keeping old grievances alive in their demands for a day of final reckoning, and he demonstrates that totalitarian and imperial regimes have made effective use of apocalyptic literature to justify their own violence and to terrify their subjects and enemies.

For Robert MacLennan, Friend

Dreams of Glory
The Sources of Apocalyptic Terror

RICHARD K. FENN
Princeton Theological Seminary, USA

ASHGATE

Published by
Ashgate Publishing Limited
Gower House
Croft Road
Aldershot
Hampshire GU11 3HR
England

Ashgate Publishing Company
Suite 420
101 Cherry Street
Burlington, VT 05401-4405
USA

Ashgate website: http://www.ashgate.com

British Library Cataloguing in Publication Data
Fenn, Richard K.
   Dreams of glory: the sources of apocalyptic terror
   1. Fundamentalism – United States 2. Eschatology 3. Religion and politics – United States – 4. Terrorism – Religious aspects – Christianity 5. Apocalyptic literature – History and criticism 6. Religion and international affairs 7. United States – Foreign relations – Philosophy
   I. Title
   280.4'0973'09051

Library of Congress Cataloging-in-Publication Data
Fenn, Richard K.
   Dreams of glory: the source of apocalyptic terror/Richard K. Fenn.
      p. cm.
   Includes bibliographical references and index.
   ISBN 0-7546-5450-8 (hardcover: alk. paper)
   1. Apocalyptic literature—History and criticism. 2. End of the world—Comparative studies. 3. Terrorism—Religious aspects. 4. Civilization, Modern—21st century. I. Title.

BL501.F46 2005
202'.3—dc22

2005006172

ISBN 0 7546 5450 8

Typeset by Tradespools, Chippenham, Wiltshire
Printed and bound by Antony Rowe, Chippenham, Wiltshire

Contents

Contents

Acknowledgements

This book is dedicated to Robert MacLennan, whose extraordinary capacity to engage and question the sacred have enriched our friendship and conversations over many years. He is a gift not only to the church but to all those attempting to find common ground beneath religious difference.

A few years ago I had lunch with Michael Wood, who introduced me to the problem of understanding why it is that people may be troubled by possibilities even when they know the outcome in advance. That conversation has haunted me in the writing of this book, and so, rather than a single footnote to that conversation, I am thanking Michael Wood here for setting in motion a train of thought that has not begun to reach its destination but has to stop somewhere. This book is that station, but not yet, thanks to Michael Wood, a terminal.

James Moorhead, who knows more about apocalypticism than anyone else I know, is also a dear friend and colleague, whose conversations always remind me of how hard and necessary it is to keep the end in sight, even when neither of us wants to. He is steadfast, illuminating, and always kind.

I also want to thank another indispensable colleague, Sally Brown, for an invitation to think and talk about last things. She has brought intellectual honesty, depth, and rigor to our conversations, along with a compassion that always makes me wonder if I have yet even begun to understand what it is like to live in a world where nothing lasts. I can only hope that her voice will be heard for years to come.

Acknowledgements

This book is dedicated to Robert MacLennan whose extraordinary capacity to engage and illuminate the issues I have explored.

Contemporary Christian Mullahs and Their Apocalypticism

Many are rightly concerned about the apocalyptic fervor that infects American politics in the twenty-first century. A global crusade against evil, in which victory is always imminent, strikes critics of the Republican administration as a fantasy that will come to grief on the very hard soil of Iraq and the Middle East. It is a fantasy, however, that dies hard. Apocalyptic hopes and fears have been driving American politics at least since the great Awakening of the 1700s, initiated in New England by the Northampton preacher Jonathan Edwards, who scared his flock to death with visions of hell. In the movement that followed evangelists drew tens of thousands of souls eager to be saved from damnation. As the American historian Stephen D. O'Leary describes this 'Awakening':

> this was a 'moment of madness' – a revolutionary, romantic moment when an entire society seems to be up for grabs. In these moments, fundamental change appears irresistible; for a brief moment, 'all seems possible, all within reach'. Across time, people who get caught up in moments of madness imagine that their own 'radiant vision' is at hand: a workers' paradise, a grassroots democracy, fraternite-egalite-liberte, or the Second Coming of Jesus. The utopian imagination is – suddenly, powerfully, briefly – inflamed by the immediate prospect of radical change, by visions of an apocalypse now.[1]

Even among Protestant churches that are historically suspicious of enthusiasm, the apocalyptic vision is like a black hole that draws everything into itself. To be sure, Presbyterians, for instance, understand that they should never speculate on how or when the Kingdom of God will come. Rather, they must live like 'the One who participates already in God's eschatological Kingdom.'[2] That means that evil is to be confronted and revealed in everyday life, without waiting for the End or speculating on the time that remains before its final advent. Thus Christians live between a time that is not yet come and one that has already begun: a perennial, continuous, mundane, existential, and fateful way of life that intensifies the pressure of the past and the future on the present. Even so, however, orthodox belief still insists on a different fate for those who adhere to Christianity from those who do not. Many are called, but relatively few will finally be chosen.

I am not speaking merely of the extent to which conservative Christians have been able to impose their views on the administration of health and welfare in the USA and elsewhere on such specific issues as the rights of women to information regarding abortion or the right of the gay community to have their needs publicly addressed. Certainly, the more evangelical and fundamentalist Christians have politicized articles of faith, and it is now becoming clearer how powerful and potentially ruinous are the vindictive and triumphal aspects of the Christian faith. I am speaking, and will be speaking throughout this book, about the false innocence of churches that entertain views of the end of history in which the Christian faith will dominate what is left of the world. Not only do these views bias American policy in the Middle East heavily toward Israel; they legitimate the worst fears of the Islamic world.

Like their more liberal counterparts in the Islamic world, the theologians and leaders of the more mainstream and liberal Protestant denominations have yet to say, once and for all, that the time has come to get rid of the apocalyptic beliefs that legitimate fanaticism. I do not mean simply an apology for the excesses of the Church, when it has given apocalyptic blessings to the work of inquisitors and conquistadors. More is required than an apology for threatening the faithful with the fires of hell by publicly burning heretics alive. More is required than public remorse for the genocidal excesses of conquistadors who justified mass murder in the 'new world' by imagining themselves as the agents of apocalyptic purification. Until the churches repudiate the apocalyptic beliefs that have long given mass murderers a good conscience and the blessings of the Church, they continue to legitimate the excesses of conviction.

It is too easy to denounce the radical right in the USA for keeping alive the most chauvinistic, nationalistic, violent, and apocalyptic aspects of the Christian faith. It is also far too easy for liberal theologians to propose existential or pragmatic reinterpretations of the apocalyptic literature which turn the fight with Satanic forces into a continuous, personal, and mundane process. So long as apocalyptic beliefs retain the color of orthodoxy, Pat Robertson and others will use them to foment enthusiasm for a final clean-up campaign against the enemies of God.

Like Augustine, Robertson sees the world as a contest between two historical forces or 'cities,' one serving the devil, the other God.[3] Unlike Augustine, he does not have to wait until the end of time to find out who has been on the side of the devil; he already knows who's who at

Armageddon. Pat Robertson views the world as a cosmic battle pitting 'the people of the Babylonian humanistic and occultic traditions' against 'the people of the Abrahamic, monotheistic tradition.'[4] In the end, there can be no doubt that the only people left on the last day will be the few whose thoughts, words, and deeds conform to what Robertson has in mind when he speaks of the 'Abrahamic' tradition. Even these, like the Jews who survive Armageddon and the tribulations at the end of time, will have become Christians. Robertson's God will be all in all.

There is no need to insist that countries like Saudi Arabia and Egypt should silence their own clergy's rhetoric of apocalyptic hatred, so long as Pat Robertson and Jerry Falwell preach that America, as the pre-eminent Christian nation and the leader of the civilized world, has an apocalyptic duty to perform. The Christian right believes that, to fulfill the biblical promises to Israel, the USA must engage in a world-saving battle: the sooner the better, since the faithful are getting tired of waiting for their promised satisfactions. Blasphemous as such a view may seem, Pat Robertson and Jerry Falwell have given their blessing to the first-use of devastating, genocidal weapons. Using the biblical notion of an apocalyptic battle between good and evil to justify their desire to see such a final incineration, they have 'hinted that use of atomic weapons was inevitable as part of the final battle of Armageddon:' a battle that might well be fast approaching.[5] Now that there is an Islamic bomb, precariously controlled for the time being by an ally of the USA, the chances are vastly improved that the religious right in that country will have their wish for an atomic, indeed an apocalyptic, showdown.

Indeed, the Christian right's sanctioning of a pre-emptive nuclear strike against the enemies of God makes it all the more likely that terrorists will use a dirty bomb to make an American city uninhabitable for generations. The longings of the religious right for a world showdown, in which the USA, with the aid of nuclear arms, will come out as the triumphant leader of the surviving nations, makes it possible for other nations to contemplate a nuclear confrontation as if the idea could be entertained by people with a claim to some measure of rationality or simple decency.

Few, if any, are reminding us that in a nuclear holocaust, nothing will stand. If the world's arsenal of such weapons is actually used, the planet itself will become uninhabitable. That may seem an obvious point, but it took time for it to become widely recognized at the beginning of the nuclear age during the 1950s. At first, the popular imagination was stimulated by films that continued to portray an 'atomic holocaust or plague' in ways that suggested that it might have 'a cleansing quality' for the survivors; the world could be made new again.[6] The metaphor of the plague suggested that the dream of a saving remnant still survived, despite the reality of nuclear-age annihilation. In the 1950s and 1960s, it slowly became more apparent that there would be no survivors, no saving remnant, in a global nuclear war. Bomb shelters might enable individuals to survive the initial blast, but only long enough to die slowly from radiation sickness and the long winter night that would surely follow for years afterward. Only the apocalyptic imagination can still entertain the fantasy of redemptive survival.

It is clear from the rhetoric of televangelists like Robertson and Falwell that much of that earlier realism has been lost. The Christian right continues to harbor the illusion of a saving remnant consisting of the true Christians and of the converted survivors of Israel's Armageddon. They alone will prevail and live to see the final day of a heavenly earth ruled by the messianic people. An apocalyptic imagination, once relevant to earlier periods in which people sought to cope with devastating social change and with the prospect of further loss and dislocation, leaves a legacy of delusion about the chances of survival. In the wake of a nuclear or atomic war, however, there will not even be a collective memory in which to enshrine the dead or to honor their sacrifices.

Oddly, the fundamentalist Christians have become the last spiritual Darwinists. Holding that only the spiritually fit will survive a nuclear holocaust, they are in fact asserting that the outcome of Armageddon on the nuclear battlefield will favor the religious evolution of the planet. Many on the Christian and Islamic right remain to be convinced that there will be nothing and nobody left after a nuclear conflagration, except for the few spiritual survivalists that represent the *avant-garde* of the New Age.

Pat Robertson and Pat Buchanan give voice to more orthodox Christian yearnings and fears regarding the end of time. Robertson knows how to convey a picture of world events as coming to a climax in our lifetimes, as Israel and America finally fulfill biblical prophecies of the triumph of good over evil. Buchanan knows how to convey the fear of many that something is rotten in the American republic and that it is dying from internal weakness and corruption. Together they orchestrate a chorus of apprehension and vengeful longings that cannot wait to demonstrate that the United States of America alone will stand the test of time. Extreme though they are, they nevertheless have the courage of mainstream Protestant convictions about an apocalyptic end of time.

These apocalyptic beliefs do have consequences. The re-election of George W. Bush in 2004 came as no surprise to those who monitored his evangelical support in the presidential election of 2000. Except for the Jewish community, the highest rates of turnout in 2000 were among Southern white evangelicals who attended church frequently.[7] (The

Southern white evangelicals who attended less often had some of the lowest turnout rates in the nation.) In these last two elections, three-quarters of Southern evangelicals who regularly attended church also voted Republican. For the Republican Party in the South, this cadre of politicized evangelicals in 2000 accounted for 41% of their vote, and outside the South these same voters racked up 21% of the Republican vote (Green 2003: 5).

If church-going evangelicals who believe in the end of time and in America's sovereign and saving role among the nations of the earth vote in such numbers, it is because the churches are telling them to do so. As in the 2004 election, so in the campaign of 2000, evangelical churches themselves not only urged their members to vote but gave them fairly precise instructions on whom to vote for as the party of God (Green 2003: 6). For their members who may be inclined to think differently or vote for Democrats, they offer disapproval that borders on intimidation.

However, until the liberal and moderate churches, both Protestant and Catholic, renounce Christianity's apocalyptic vision of a bloody and vindictive collective exorcism, they will have nothing to say about the militant and self-destructive aspects either of the Christian right or of their Islamic counterparts. There will always be a need for Osama bin Ladens so long as the Christian churches keep apocalyptic visions alive in scripture and liturgy and in prophecies and hymns about trampling out the vineyards where the grapes of wrath are stored. Until and unless Christianity gives up its own dreams of apocalyptic glory, there will quite literally be no basis for an enduring accord with Islam. I am therefore calling for unilateral theological disarmament on the part of all the Christian churches.

The task of persuasion will not be easy. After all these centuries of conquest and even genocidal warfare, Christians still give an honored place to their apocalyptic literature. Not only do triumphalist tracts like the Revelation of John still remain in the Scriptures, but there is also an immensely popular literature of apocalyptic rebuke and speculation, such as Hal Lindsey's apocalyptic scenario, *The Late Great Planet Earth* (1970). Consider this relatively harmless excerpt from Lindsey's reminiscence of a scene at the shore:

> You know, I used to come to the beach to get away from things. Just the relaxing of the waves pounding the shore. But now even the ocean is a reminder that man may be running out of time. Scientists tell us today that we are approaching a time when the ocean may not be able to sustain life anymore. The Secretary General of the UN recently told us that man has perhaps ten years to solve the problem of survival.[8]

The ocean, which should always be a source of nourishment for the planet, is becoming poisonous.

For Lindsey and others infected with an apocalyptic viewpoint, it is the world, and more particularly our social world, that is polluted. Families and neighborhoods, schools and even churches, certainly the world of work and politics, all suffer from the intrusion of external influences. For the fundamentalist Christian, secular humanism is ruining a traditional way of life, the state is intruding on the local community, foreign influences are polluting the nation, and agencies like the United Nations are impeding the exercise of national sovereignty. For the Islamic fundamentalist, it is American culture that is infecting the youth, foreign capital that is impoverishing the local farmer and merchant, and a secular state that is undermining the control of Islamic tradition. To some it might seem that, for such total corruption, there can only be an apocalyptic solution. Instead, I am arguing that the apocalyptic imagination itself makes the world seem to need a cosmic purification in a final exorcism of ethnic and religious cleansing. It is long past the time when the churches should have apologized for the consequences of this poisonous vision of the future, but it is not too late to prevent that vision from causing further and wholly irreversible damage.

Although Lindsey draws heavily on his updated reading of the Book of Revelation in the New Testament and the Book of Daniel in the Old Testament, he is in fact drawing on ancient residues of the apocalyptic imagination that were common in the Near and Middle East. Long before the rise of Zoroastrianism or Hinduism, Indo-European myths spoke of a battle to ensure that the waters would return and renew the earth's power to nourish and support life. Standing in the way of these essential waters, however, was always a beast that must yet be destroyed. Otherwise, life would not go on, and time would indeed run out. Drawing on the imagery of the beast in the Book of Daniel, Lindsey rounds up the usual suspects: Babylon and Persia, Greece and Rome, who hold the sceptre of world rule (Lindsey 1970: 105–6). Here again we have the familiar picture of the world divided between two forces, East and West. His is a demonic image of a world order that defies the dictates of Scripture and the will of God. Against the rule of blasphemy there is only one antidote: a world dominated by the people of God. According to Lindsey (1970: 109ff.), during the time immediately before the advent of the Christian millennium, there will be 144,000 Jews with the fervor and faith of Billy Graham evangelizing the world in the name of Christ (Lindsey 1970: 111). These Jewish evangelists for Christ 'are going to make up for lost time' (Lindsey 1970: 111). Their preaching will extend outward in all directions from the

Holy Land, but they will still be faced with the overwhelming power of the one whom Lindsey calls a Roman Dictator, the Antichrist.

So long as drastic social changes and defeats in battle continue, it will seem to many of Lindsey's readers as if their world is indeed coming to an end. For this reason alone, there will always be some who find in Lindsey's popular apocalyptic vision a way to imagine that the end of suffering is near, and that they will soon enjoy their own triumph and revenge. However, this story, recently updated by the likes of Lindsey and the authors of the *Left Behind* series of apocalyptic novels, is as old as that in Matthew 24:41ff:

> So will it be at the coming of the Son of Man. Two men will be in the field; one is taken and one is left behind. Two women will be grinding at the hand mill; one is taken and one is left behind. You must be on the alert then, because you do not know when your master is coming.

The world will be divided on the last day into two parts, and one will be left behind forever, to languish in obscurity and torment.

I mention these verses from Matthew 24 because they are a standard part of the lectionary of the mainstream Protestant as well as Catholic churches during the season of Advent, the weeks leading up to the holiday of Christmas. How can Episcopalians and Presbyterians sneer at the *Left Behind* series of novels, when that same vision informs their own readings from Scripture at the start of the church year?

Granted that few mainstream churches show movies to their young people in which children come home from school to find no one there, but the motor still running on the lawn mower in the back yard. Such films have frightened at least two generations of children, and I have had the privilege of meeting a few of them at the seminary where I teach. When they are being candid, they will admit that for years after seeing such a film they lived in terror of losing their mothers in the Rapture prior to the Second Coming of Christ, and of being thus left behind. To inspire such terror, or 'holy fear,' is one function of the apocalyptic vision itself. Thus, when the churches envisage a Day of Wrath, a dreadful judgment at the end of time, the marriage of innocence to sacralized destruction is consummated not in the liturgy but in a final orgy of violence, in which the innocent have the infinite satisfaction of seeing the wicked suffer unspeakable torments. It is as if the innocent are not really there, although they can witness the carnage, and it is not they who are doing it but the divine hand.

To fight terrorism with religiously inspired terror is to lose the battle before it begins. Terrorism has the capacity to make people believe that anything can happen anywhere at any time. That is why acts of terrorism are so powerful. However, apocalyptic visions arouse the very same sense of unspeakable possibility. In fact, apocalyptic beliefs turn paranoia into an article of faith and demand a day of final reckoning. Pat Robertson, for instance, reassures his followers that it is going to be all right with God if the United States loves its enemy, Osama bin Laden, by taking him 'out of circulation.' That is because 'The Bible makes it clear that God is on the side of established order.'[9] As for Christians, if they love their Lord, they have nothing to fear, because they are guaranteed eternal life. Muslims, on the other hand, no matter how devout they are in their worship of Allah, can never live or die with such an assurance. Those with such an eternal advantage are of course obligated not to keep it to themselves but to share it with a hungry world, and Robertson therefore assures his followers that Muslims are seeking Jesus by the millions (Robertson 2003: 273).

There is a catch. Unless Americans repent their sinful ways and ask God for help in reforming their personal and national lives, God will abandon them to their enemies. That is because Americans have allowed God to be eliminated from the schools and workplaces, from the courts and the media, of the country. Even worse, Americans have been on a binge of endorsing homosexuality, adultery, fornication, incest, various kinds of crime, and abortion: all abominations unto the Lord (Robertson 2003: 264–6). God, according to Robertson (2003: 267), will lead America to triumph over all its enemies if, and only if, Americans are good.

There is no mistaking the element of threat in this apocalyptic message. Speaking to the question, 'Did God allow the attacks on September 11?', Robertson (2003: 266) says, 'I believe that the protection, the covering of God that has been on this great land of ours for so many years, had lifted on September 11, and allowed this thing to happen.' God apparently had good reasons for exposing the USA to such destruction, given the many sins that Americans have committed ever since the Roe versus Wade court case and the Supreme Court's decision to keep God out of the schools. In fact, American infidelity goes back to the 1920s and 1930s, to situational ethics and notions of cultural relativity, along with a flirtation with communism at the highest levels of government. The point is not just that Americans have been bad and forfeited their entitlements. It is that unless they reform themselves in a hurry, something far worse may happen to them.

There is also no mistaking the attempt to use apocalyptic imagery to terrify people into repentance and submission. Robertson (2003: 265) regards September 11 as 'a wake-up call,' and there will be 'worse calamities coming if we don't repent and turn to Him.' Homeland security depends on piety, as defined by the Christian right. Is it fanciful to imagine that, after the next major attack on America, Robertson and the Christian right will call for the isolation and punishment of such conspicuous sinners as those who practice abortion and homosexuality? We already know that some on the Christian right think that their faith gives them a license to kill doctors who perform abortions.

Until and unless the mainstream churches disavow themselves not only of these extreme interpretations of the Christian revelation but of apocalyptic doctrine itself, they will continue to provide an umbrella for this sort of Christian terrorism.

Christian terrorism? Am I not being a bit extreme here? Consider Robertson (2003) again:

> It is logical to assume that any nation that has willingly slaughtered more than forty million innocent unborn babies, as we have done in the United States, would be subject to the wrath of God. Indeed, any nation that has practiced sodomy, adultery, fornication, and all manner of debauchery, as we in America have done *should live in terror* [emphasis added] not from Islamic fanatics, but *terror at what Almighty God will do when His patience is exhausted.*

This is not the raving of a lunatic preacher. It is simply a rather literal interpretation of the apocalyptic vision contained in the Bible and prayer books of mainstream Protestants and Catholics.

What could possibly convince the Christian and Islamic aficionados of the apocalypse to lay down their own dreams of triumph and revenge, so long as the churches themselves claim that the books of history will not be balanced until there is such a day of final accounting? It is hopeless to ask Islam to renounce its own apocalyptic beliefs until the Christian community has itself first abandoned its own longings for a day of triumph and revenge.

It is not enough for theologians, Muslim or Christian, to insist that the apocalypse is a continuing process, or a state of mind, or an existential metaphor, and that the Last Judgment, begun long ago, is always and everywhere impinging on each person in every moment. That may be true. If it *is* true, it is due to the secularizing impulses in Christianity and in Islam alike, in which the temporal is imbued with the eternal, and the eternal is put to the test of time. Thus the Kingdom of God is always and everywhere a way of life into which individuals may enter, but it is not identified with any particular community or nation, state or political system. Similarly, as Talal Asad points out, the Islamic *umma* is not what modern thought might consider a society, let alone a nation.[10] But like the Christian Kingdom of God, it is a world and a way of life that exists in its own right, on its own terms, and which impinges on every individual. The Kingdom and the *umma* are aspects of eternity that imbue the temporal with essential life and meaning. Such a belief requires all Muslims and Christians to work out their faiths in the secular world where time passes, and where space always gives way to time. That is why Christian and Islamic apocalyptic beliefs will always tend to take secular form. No wonder, then, that secularists wish to keep religion from having too much success in secularizing itself (Asad 2003: 199–200).

There is much to be said for a continuous, this-worldly version of the apocalypse that brings suffering to light, creates an awareness of the unique and unprecedented in human history, and opens the way to a future that will not perpetuate the ills of the past but will be in fact, as well as in promise, a new age. Similarly, there is indeed much to be said for Islamic notions of 'progress toward a fuller understanding of God ... in this world through the living of a morally upright life, so the abodes of the next are viewed by many as the arena of constant movement upward toward higher states of bliss, knowledge, and ultimate contemplation of the divine itself' (Smith and Haddad 2002: 146). This story of progress is clearly on the agenda of the leaders who are the subject of Smith and Haddad's review of Islamic hopes for the End, just as they are on the agenda of the moderate Presbyterians who subscribe to the notion that 'God's love ... is transforming us even now ... [and that] God's purpose will indeed be brought to consummation.'[11]

However, unless these apocalyptic traditions can be successfully secularized into notions of societal progress and personal fulfillment, they will continue to provide a very short fuse for the explosive tensions that are accumulating within and between Christian, Jewish, and Islamic societies. Apocalyptic visions are dangerous because they are self-fulfilling. They virtually ensure that the future will tend to repeat the cataclysms of past conflicts in which wars destroyed the cities of what we now call the Near and Middle East. These cities were entire symbolic worlds, and their loss was experienced as a cosmic devastation. The current East–West conflict is thus a deeply rooted, civil war within a civilization that links Persia and Greece with Israel and Rome and with their descendants in the modern world.

Both Christianity and Islam draw their apocalyptic visions from the same sources in the world of Hellenistic, Persian, and Greco-Roman antiquity. These are sources with long memories and a merciless determination to take revenge. Unless the apocalyptic vision is eliminated, or at least radically secularized, the civil war between Islamic and Christian peoples is likely to come to an end very much in the same way that it began, that is, in a futile and suicidal attempt to eliminate outstanding differences.

Notes

1 In James A. Morone, *Hellfire Nation: The Politics of Sin in American Society*. New Haven and London: Yale University Press, 2003, p. 108.
2 'Eschatology: The Doctrine of Last Things' (1978), quoted in *Between Millennia: What Presbyterians Believe About the Coming of Christ*, a publication of the Office of Theology and Worship, The Presbyterian Church (USA), 2001, p. 5.
3 See J. LeGoff, *History and Memory*, translated by Steven Rendall and Elizabeth Claman. New York: Columbia University Press, 1992, p. 155.
4 Pat Robertson, *The New World Order*. Dallas: Word Publishing, 1991, p. 258.
5 Chip Berlet and Matthew N. Lyons, *Right-Wing Populism in America: Too Close for Comfort*. New York and London: The Guilford Press, 2000, pp. 325–6.
6 Stephen D. O'Leary, 'Popular Culture and Apocalypticism,' in *The Encyclopedia of Apocalypticism*, Vol. 3, *Apocalypticism in the Modern Period and the Contemporary Age*, edited by Stephen J. Stein. New York: Continuum Publishing, 2000, p. 410.
7 John C. Green, 'The Undetected Tide,' *Religion in the News*, Spring 2003, Hartford, Conn.: Trinity College, pp. 4–7.
8 Hal Lindsey, with C.C. Carlson, *The Late Great Planet Earth*. Grand Rapids, Mich.: Zondervan Publishing, 1970, frontal page.
9 Pat Robertson, *Bring It On: Tough Questions, Candid Answers*. Nashville, Tennessee: W Publishing Group, 2003, p. 267.
10 Talal Asad, *Formations of the Secular: Christianity, Islam, and Modernity*. Stanford, California: Stanford University Press, 2003, p. 197ff.
11 'Eschatology: The Doctrine of Last Things' (1978), quoted in *Between Millennia: What Presbyterians Believe About the Coming of Christ*, a publication of the Office of Theology and Worship, The Presbyterian Church (USA), 2001, p. 7.

CHAPTER 1

The Apocalyptic Vision as Bad Seed

From *The New York Times*, September 28, 2004, after the Chechnyan rebels had left over three hundred dead, many of them children, in a school in Beslan, Russia:

> Every morning, Vova Tumayev sets the breakfast table for three – husband, wife and adored 10-year-old daughter. Nobody eats. Mr. Tumayev sits alone for a little while, then clears the table.
>
> His wife, Zinaida, and his daughter, Madina, died in the seizure of a schoolhouse here at the beginning of September, two of the hundreds of victims of an attack linked to the war in Chechnya.
>
> There is nothing Mr. Tumayev can do – no ritual, no act of mourning that can begin to fill the emptiness their loss has left behind.
>
> At night, he said, he sleeps in his daughter's bed.
>
> 'They say "Aren't you scared to do that?"' said Mr. Tumayev, 44, a plumber. 'I say I'm not afraid of anything. But it's true, whenever I lie there some strange things come into my eyes.'
>
> As the people of this little town struggle with their grief, the schoolhouse where their children died has become a place of echoes and memories as well. Hollow and filled with rubble, it is piled with wreaths and offerings, with messages of condolence scribbled like graffiti on its walls.
>
> Mr. Tumayev is just one lonely mourner in a town where thousands of people are bereaved.
>
> He married rather late, at the age of 34, to a kindergarten teacher, and the warmth of having a family, here in this little bachelor's apartment, continued to fill him with astonishment and joy.
>
> 'I gave her everything she asked,' he said of his daughter. 'I never said no to her.'
>
> 'My wife said, "Be strict with her so she'll obey you," but I couldn't. Sometimes my wife scolded her. I never did. When I came home from work she'd run out and hug me.'
>
> Already, he said, friends are urging him to move on once the traditional mourning period is over, as if the past could possibly be left behind.

'They tell me, "After 40 days, go marry again,"' he said. 'But even if I marry again 10 times I'll never have a child like that. How I loved her, how I loved her.'

He picked them out immediately in the morgue, he said, although their bodies were charred and grotesque.

'My daughter was shot in the head,' he said. 'One leg was off, the other was barely joined to her body. Her face was so burned you couldn't recognize it. I just recognized her earrings, and a bit of her hair, and immediately I knew it was my daughter.'

'People were saying, "Maybe it's not her,"' he said. 'They had numbers on them, and I said, "Write that number down." I knew them right away.'

Mr. Tumayev has set up a little shrine at home, a table piled with bananas, apples, dried fruits, biscuits, and his daughter's favorite sweets.

His apartment is filled with pictures of her, just as the walls of the schoolhouse are pasted with photographs of missing children – each one a reminder of her absence.

He took a small album of photographs from a shelf and began turning its pages one by one, explaining each picture to a visitor as he went.

'That's her,' he said, showing a picture of a smiling girl in a red dress. 'That's her, that's her, that's her at the beach; that's also her and here she is, here she is, here, here she is; there she is in the countryside, there also, and that's her, too.'

'Oof, this is difficult,' he said, but he kept turning the pages.

'There she is in Rostov, there she is, too; there she is with her mother; there she is, she was tall, almost as tall as me; that's her, too, and that's her, too, and that's her, and that's also her, also her, also her; there she is with her friends, that little girl died, too, there she is waving.'

'Everything in here is her,' he said, handing the album to his visitor. 'I don't want to look anymore.'[1]

There are many kinds of moments; if this one does not represent the worst, it is close enough. Mr. Tumayev has experienced a total rupture in his life, an abrupt loss of everything that made him want to live. He knows that there is no way to recover his daughter, no matter how many times he marries, because she was unique. There will be no second chance, no repeat of the joy of being greeted by her when he comes home from work. He has lost what was and remains to him essential, and she is present only under the signs of her absence. The photographs in the album, no matter how often he points to her, cannot make her presence real, and the domestic shrine, like the places set for his wife and daughter at meal time, brings home his loss. The commentators who tell him to 'move on,' although they are Russian, sound like Americans advising someone to get on with his life. The newspaperman's comment about the futility of the father's rituals seems gratuitous. Most readers, I believe, would sense the emptiness of these grief-filled gestures without being so instructed by the reporter. The moment that Mr. Tumayev has endured beggars commentary.

When confronted by such a moment, reporters and editors, like the scribes that tried to make sense of the many moments in the life of Jesus of Nazareth, are seldom at a loss for words. They find a precedent for the unprecedented or look forward to a later moment that will put the present in some meaningful perspective. Mr. Tumayev's friends tell him to move on and remarry; there will be better days, in the light of which this one will not seem to be so total an end of everything that makes life possible. Rather than a total break between the present and either the past or the future, this current moment will turn out to have been like a chapter in a book. Just to talk about it helps to move the catastrophe of loss into the magic kingdom of narrative. What seemed to be the end of everything will turn out to have been an incident, however horrendous, in a larger story.

Even to speak of Mr. Tumayev with expressions such as 'moments like this' tends to make his moment less tragic or even apocalyptic. Mr. Tumayev knows what it means to have everything come to an end. He cannot look any more at the pictures because that is precisely what they say: that his life is over, yet he still lives, however miserably and without hope. There is nothing to be done about it. There is no way to have prevented the end of everything; no way Mr. Tumayev could have saved his family, and no way for him now to do anything about his condition, surrounded as he is by reminders of his irreversible loss and of death itself. All that is left is the ticking of the clock: one moment after another, with no connection among the moments, no continuity or development, and nothing left to be said or done. It is what Stephen O'Leary, speaking of the apocalypse, has called 'the locus of the irreparable.'[2] Less grandly stated, it is hell.

In what Stephen O'Leary calls 'the tragic apocalyptic program' there is unrepeatable and irreversible loss: 'the list of ills only serves to prove that the end of history is imminent and unavoidable.'[3] Certainly, there is something apocalyptic, irreparably final, about the moment in which Mr. Tumayev lost both his family and the future. Do his well-meaning friends understand this, in their attempts to tell him that he will have other children and that it is soon time to move on? No other future can be generated to replace the one that he has lost forever. Promises of a better day have become meaningless. There will never come a day when he will see again the one person who made every day worth living. The apocalypse is the end of time; there is no future in it.

To lose the future is to lose any way of imagining and projecting oneself; it is in this sense like death itself. Michel de Montaigne speaks of just such a moment in the life of Charles de Guise, then (circa 1572) Cardinal de Lorraine:

> He was at Trent: first he heard the news of the death of his very special elder brother, the support and pride of his whole family; then came the death of his younger brother, their second hope. He bore both these blows with exemplary fortitude; yet, when a few days later one of his men happened to die, he let himself be carried away by this event; he abandoned his resolute calm and gave himself over to grief and sorrow – so much so that some argued that only this last shock had touched him to the quick. The truth is that he was already brimful of sadness, so the least extra burden broke down the barriers of his endurance.[4]

The Cardinal had lost the future, the two brothers who were the hope and support of the family; no wonder that he was 'brimful of sadness.' Such a loss makes it virtually impossible to imagine one's own life going on, as if one were looking in a mirror without seeing any reflection at all. De Montaigne goes on to say that 'The force of extreme sadness inevitably stuns the whole of our soul, impeding her freedom of action.'[5] A loss too deep for words throws the soul back on the memory of what it was like, as an infant, when you were unable to imagine how you could wait another minute for the saving presence of someone else. As an infant, you may also have felt as if you were wholly at a loss for words, unable to shout or speak in a way that would command a response to your anguish. In such a moment, as de Montaigne puts it, 'we are enraptured, seized, paralysed in all our movements in such a way that, afterwards, when the soul lets herself go with tears and lamentations, she seems to have struggled loose, disentangled herself and become free to range about as she wishes.'[6] Visions of the apocalypse speak of a day when there will be no further need for such tears, and the soul will remain forever enthralled, either by horror or joy. In the apocalypse lost moments of intense anguish return, whether to bring punishment or release, but in either event, there will be no future.

Apocalyptic beliefs can have the unprecedented and unpredictable consequences that open the world to terror. As the horror of Beslan, Russia, has reminded us, there is no safe haven to protect the citizen from apocalyptic terror and terrorism. Not even the nation-state can protect its citizens from the forces that destroy traditional communities and their ways of life. Floods of money and people, ideas and music, may invade any neighborhood and even the home, turning the generations against each other. The global economy is becoming increasingly potent and invasive. Many Americans therefore fear that 'The laws and rules that govern the global order and are instituted by the new world government will take precedence over the federal government of the United States, and Americans will be taking orders from foreigners' (Lamy 1997: 104). In such a world, people stare into the future and cannot find any sign of themselves and their ways of life; even their children will have turned their backs while singing the songs of foreigners. It is thus understandable that many are holding on to apocalyptic beliefs for guidance in a world that is no longer familiar or secure, even when those beliefs fuel terror itself.

The state, even as it expands into the lives of local communities and individuals, nonetheless fails to protect them from outside influences. Like the Roman beast in the Book of Revelation, sacrificing local communities to the goddess Roma, modern states make local communities pay taxes and tribute, while requiring human sacrifice for the sake of a global market. That is why outsourcing is a major political issue in the USA; communities are decimated when jobs go overseas. For the same reason, meetings of the World Bank and the International Monetary Fund face protesters in the streets who seek to protect local farmers in Africa and Asia from the cheaper farm goods flowing into the community from rich nations.

In one of the debates leading up to the presidential elections of 2004 in the USA, John Kerry, the Democratic candidate for president, said that American foreign policy would have to face 'a global test.' What he meant was that every effort should be made to secure international support for American initiatives, or at the very least international understanding, before embarking on initiatives to defend the nation against a variety of foreign threats. However, his opponents seized the opportunity to portray Mr. Kerry as someone who would sacrifice American sovereignty and thus expose Americans to the very threats from which the state is supposed to protect them. Neither Mr. Kerry nor his opponent, however, were willing to acknowledge that the millions being spent on national security cannot deter all terrorists, like those who left Mr. Tumayev and many others in Beslan, Russia, without a future.

In the USA there is a long tradition of hostility to outside influences. Sometimes these have been portrayed as Catholic, with immigrants polluting America with subversive and un-American loyalties; at other times the influences have been imagined as Jewish, notably international bankers or communists who suck the life-blood from American workers and households. More recently, the Christian right has imagined secular humanists, civil libertarians, homosexuals, and feminists to be part of an international conspiracy that includes Muslims and terrorists: all seeking to thwart the sovereignty of the USA and to distract America from its providential assignment to bring the nations of the world to their democratic, and Christian, senses. For any presidential candidate to suggest that American foreign policy could be subject to international approval would therefore be seen as a peculiar mixture of heresy and treason. The values of families and local communities are being subverted by elites who in the past have sought to secularize their children's education, require them to go to school with blacks, tolerate homosexuals, undermine the authority of their parents, and allow immigrants from Central and Latin America to take away their parents' jobs.

Like conservative Christians, Islamic conservatives have also found a new world order dominated by secular humanists and foreign governments to be hostile to their own traditional beliefs and values. Not surprisingly, therefore, Islamic apocalyptic literature offers hope for a world purified of alien influence and corruption through cosmic battle and sacrifice. For instance, in Iran, prior to the Iranian revolution, oppressed groups of farmers and merchants were being overwhelmed by global social and economic changes. Understandably, they were opposed to the new world order and wished the nation to defend its citizens against the intrusion of foreign people, foreign ideas, and foreign capital. The Shah imposed his rule in ways that directly affected communal life and also offended traditional religion, and a globally oppressed class of believers longed for liberation, vindication, and revenge. A state opposed to traditional religious leaders alienated the clergy, who in their turn have become unresponsive to the needs of the people and impotent to help them. Under these conditions, religious ideology radically redefined the relationships among all contenders in the struggle for power and fostered the Islamic fundamentalist movement in Iran under Ayatollah Khomeini.[7]

So long as Muslims and Christians entertain apocalyptic beliefs, the drive toward Armageddon will continue. While some are strapping bombs to their bodies, others are driving trucks filled with explosives into the places where 'the enemy' gathers or concentrates its strength and resources. Whether the target is the federal building in Oklahoma City or the World Trade Center in New York, the goal is to purify the world of alien influences and to restore control to the local community. To deprive apocalyptic beliefs of their terror is therefore the first line of defense against terrorism.

Despite the growth of apocalyptic movements hell bent on terrorizing or on achieving global supremacy, some commentators have looked on them as a bit of an anomaly in the modern world. Consider Nicholas Kristof's review of a book by Robert J. Lifton on the apocalyptic cult Aum Shinrikyo, which had tried to gas subway passengers in Tokyo in an attack that killed few but injured thousands more. Lifton had argued that the long-term effects of the cult were yet to be measured, since the cult leader had initiated a new age of terror with weapons that could slaughter literally millions. Kristof argued that:

> Millenary cults have been around for millenniums, and it seems unlikely that any new guru will prove as deadly as the man in mid-19th-century China who proclaimed himself the younger brother of Jesus and led the Taiping rebellion. That uprising resulted in the deaths of countless millions of people and contributed to the collapse of imperial China. And it would take quite a remarkable effort to match the biological weapons of the European settlers in America. Their introduction of smallpox—mainly by accident but also by use of deliberately infected blankets—helped wipe out much of the native population in the New World.[8]

Like Mr. Kristof, since September 11, 2001 and the demonstration of Osama bin Laden's effective management of mass murder, many of us have had to give the millennial question a second thought. Now we are in a situation that, for many Americans, seems not only new but unprecedented. It is a time when old scores are about to be settled on a scale that few of us have troubled to imagine since the first, frightening years after the invention of the atomic bomb. That is, after all, what an apocalypse does: it brings to light old animosities and introduces new possibilities in a time that seems, for those who suffer through it, like the beginning of the end. That is also what modernity does, whether you are living in the sixth century or the twenty-first.

There is no doubt that the bombing of the World Trade Center and the Pentagon on September 11, 2001 evoked apocalyptic images in the minds of many who suffered as well as those who merely commented on the day's events. One eyewitness account by a New York City fireman does speak of the collapsing towers as making a terrifying sound reminiscent of the devil and that the fires were like those long imagined to accompany the apocalypse at the end of time. Certainly, the descriptions of bodies falling, of smoke clouds, of horrendous fire and panicked crowds running from the horror, do evoke apocalyptic images. When the firemen protested the Mayor's decision to remove all but a small crew from the scene of the disaster, it was because the site still held the remains of many of their comrades. Since the vast majority of the firefighters were Catholic, commented one of them, their comrades could only give a church burial to those whose remains had been recovered. A part was required, if only a very small part, to signify the whole body.[9] The dead will come back to haunt the living so long as their memory is not honored and their spirits sent properly on their way to the life hereafter, and their untimely return is a staple of apocalyptic visions.

There is also no doubt that for many Americans the war on Iraq was a day of apocalyptic judgment. For some, even the soldiers, it was just 'pay-back time.' Certainly, many of the soldiers who were sent to the Iraqi front knew that, for all their professionalism, there was a very 'personal' score that had to be settled.[10] Retribution was also on the minds of all those who marked their bombs with references to September 11 and of the millions of Americans who believed that there were intimate links between Saddam Hussein and Osama bin Laden's Al Qaeda network. No doubt there were some terrorist training camps in Iraq, but it became clear during the 2004 presidential campaign that the Republican administration was really concerned about Iraq's connection with Hamas and other Palestinian groups opposing the Israeli occupation. That is, the invasion of Iraq served America's pro-Israel policies, regardless of any possible connection of Iraq either with Al Qaeda or 'weapons of mass destruction.' That so many Americans believed in the Iraqi threat to the United States, well in advance of any hard evidence to that effect, was due, I am arguing, to the profound sense that the time had come for retribution. Thus the war in Afghanistan had been not the beginning of the end but the beginning of the time of judgment.

Conservative Christians in the USA are not the only ones who are eager for Jesus to come back and settle old scores. Among Muslims there is what Gershom Gorenberg calls 'an old Islamic idea that at history's finale a Jewish Antichrist will rule until Jesus, as Muslim prophet, returns to defeat him.'[11] That idea has surfaced again in a very popular set of books by the Egyptian author Sa'id Ayyub, in which the Jewish Antichrist is not only armed with missiles but is wearing a Star of David alongside an American flag while sporting hammer and sickle: the trinity of evil. These books have received a wide readership, and for many Muslims they may be portraying the simple truth that a final showdown with Israel and America is as imminent as it is inevitable. Add to that the well-known support given by Christian evangelicals to extremists in Israel who are yearning for the day when they can destroy the Dome of the Rock and offer sacrifice in a rebuilt Temple. Like the extremists in the first century CE who plunged Israel into a disastrous civil war and destroyed Jerusalem in an attempt to purify the Temple and the holy city of all foreign presences, these extremists are tired of waiting for God.[12] There is a trilateral push, then, for a day of final reckoning, despite the fact that the end, when it comes, will be a clear holocaust.

For many American Christians, the return of Israel to the land, where Jews from various parts of the world will gather under the sovereignty of the state of Israel, is merely a prelude to the final struggle in which Jews will follow a new messiah, suffer excruciating losses, be converted to Christianity, and finally be superseded forever in the advent of the Christian millennium. For Israel, that would mean Armageddon and, at best, a very costly victory over ancient enemies. For conservative Christians, that would mean the time had come for the United States to exercise its unfettered sovereignty as the new Israel and as the lead nation of the world. For us all, it would mean mutually assured destruction, one bomb, one city at a time.

In urging the state of Israel to build a Temple on the Mount, the Christian right is thus hoping to precipitate the end. That is why not only Jewish but also Muslim experts study the archaeology of the Temple Mount in Jerusalem: not only to locate the original outlines of their own shrines but also to legitimate their claims to future occupation. The future is thus clearly intended to repeat and restore past entitlements to exclusive occupancy.

However, such moves inevitably will result in a repetition of past disasters. Remember that Ariel Sharon's visit to the Temple Mount triggered the last wave of Palestinian revolt; think what might be accomplished by an attempt to unearth the remains of – or even to rebuild – the Temple itself. Certainly, the *Left Behind* series of apocalyptic novels foresees a peace treaty between Islam and Israel that allows the Temple to be rebuilt on the Temple Mount, followed by the obligatory desecration of the Temple by the Antichrist during the apocalyptic 'tribulations.'[13]

Indeed, the Christian right may get its wishes for a time of devastating battles and horrendous losses. The Temple has already been desecrated on a number of previous occasions, most notably, for Christians, the destruction of Jerusalem in the civil war of 66–73 CE. Furthermore, there was talk, in the latter half of 2004, of the possibility of civil war in Israel itself if the government sought to dismantle and withdraw even a few of the settlements on the West Bank. As in the first century, when civil war erupted between Palestinian zealots and a government determined to keep peace with the international community, there is now a very real possibility that government troops will clash with religious zealots determined to hold on to the dream of a religious nation-state entitled to the land of a still-imagined greater Israel. Talk of Armageddon seems increasingly plausible when zealots not only become tired of waiting for national dreams to materialize, but face increasing threats not only from their gentile neighbors but from their own states. If the Israeli and Christian right-wingers are to be dissuaded from their pursuit of total ownership and control, it will only be because the Christian churches as a whole discredit, once and for all, the apocalyptic beliefs on which the Christian right bases its pretensions.

War and defeat breed hatred and humiliation, but the apocalyptic imagination keeps these emotions simmering until they boil over in brutal attacks on the innocent. Just as the 1967 war mobilized Islamic radicals, the humiliating defeat of American forces in the long war in Vietnam aroused the passions of Christian fundamentalists and conservatives in the USA during the 1970s and 1980s. The USA itself had been beaten by an army of peasants fighting their own version of a holy war. That defeat was a possibility that had not been seriously entertained by the millions of citizens who believed not only in the power, but in the rightness, of every American cause. To the conservative Christian community, it was a victory for the communists and thus for those who represented the enemies of God.

Modernity and the Apocalyptic Imagination

Why then are the moderate and relatively rational or pragmatic Christian churches adding a very dangerous fuel to the political fires now being fanned by the enthusiasm of the Islamic and Christian right? To understand the depth of apocalyptic fervor in the USA we need to go beyond the disasters of September 11 to the simple fact that there are millions of Americans who hold an apocalyptic world view, much but not all of it biblical. Not only is President Bush an evangelical Christian who feels that he is carrying out a divine mission against the 'axis of evil,' but there are also literally thousands of millennial groups armed with weapons or fortified with prayers and rituals that will augment their chances of surviving the end times. Some are Jewish, others are Mormon, Christian fundamentalist, or New Age enthusiasts fascinated with extraterrestrial signs and wonders.[14]

More important than these groups that seem to occupy the fringes of American culture or who cluster in particular urban neighborhoods are the millions of Americans who believe quite simply that their Lord and Savior will come again *during their lifetimes*. I emphasize the shortness of their time-perspective. They will live to see the day when the graves are opened, old scores are settled, the righteous triumph over the wicked and the unfaithful are consumed in the fires and earthquakes of the last days. 'The Lord Jesus is coming back! He may be here at any moment! He may come today! ... It is the sober statement of a fact, to arouse souls from their carelessness and indifference, and point them to the clear testimony of God's only Word that the Lord Jesus is coming again, and may be here today.'[15] The apocalyptic moment, however final it may be, ushers in for the faithful a timeless rapture, and if there is to be more time, it will not be like the past, the succession of *befores* and *afters*, but a millennium, in which there are no more losses, and every tear is wiped away. For the remainder, the end is quite simply torment followed by extinction.

Their expectations that the end is near may explain the high levels of recklessness that endanger the environment. Worse yet, enthusiasts for the end could use nuclear weapons in a pre-emptive strike to give the wicked a foretaste of the fires to come. In the meantime, the chosen imagine that they have some immunity from the nuclear war that is sure to come if America does not trample out the foreign vineyards where the grapes of wrath are stored.

It is therefore not surprising that social movements promising a brighter future any day now, a new millennium, so often literally come to grief. As Stephen O'Leary reminds us, the Millerite movement that later came to be called the Seventh Day Adventists expected the world to come to an end first in March 1844, and when that day proved disappointing, the Second Coming was postponed to October 22 of the same year. Many of the Millerites had given away or sold all their possessions; they had no homes to return to, so ardent was their hope for the Bridegroom to return on time. When the Bridegroom tarried yet again and they were left with nothing, they were deprived of any future at all: they had neither the one they had longed for or the one they otherwise would have had, if they had not abandoned their homes and ways of life. Together they wept all night in the keenest and most heartbroken sorrow.[16]

The apocalyptic vision, I am arguing, not only embodies the end of time but promises compensation to the faithful for lost futures. Even the dead will have the future that they had not lived long enough to see. For those who have too long wept in disappointment over futures that never arrived, the last day offers a final moment of consummation, the fulfillment of every expectation. In the years prior to the Millerite movement, O'Leary reminds us, there had been ample reason for such grief. In the 1820s and 1830s evangelists had held revivals, attacked the ills of slavery and alcoholism, and raised hopes of a day when both these demons would be exorcized from the American body politic. O'Leary is quite clear that these hopes were disappointed not only because alcoholism is not so easily cured but because slave owners put up strong moral as well as political resistance to attacks on the institution of slavery itself. Their reaction 'made an optimistic faith in the progress of future reforms seem untenable.'[17] Great expectations came to grief.

More than the expectation of moral reformation was at stake. Americans had become optimistic that their nation would progress on a number of fronts, the economic as well as the social and political. When their economic bubble burst in 1837, it was as if a future had died: 'some Americans were disposed to view current events in light of a pessimistic reading of Biblical prophecy.'[18] No wonder there were new signs everywhere of an apocalyptic day when chronic grief over a lost future would come to an end. For the faithless there will be no more future, nothing ahead for which to hope and pray, only the end of all expectation for a better day. The apocalyptic vision thus offers a compromise between hope and despair.

The apocalyptic vision trains people to expect more from the moment than life ordinarily is able to give. To believe that the Lord may come at any time, even though the day and hour of his coming are perennially uncertain, puts believers in the middle of a chronic purgatory, always on the lookout for whatever sin might delay the advent of bliss. O'Leary says as much of the effect of the apocalyptic expectations that survived the collapse of the Millerite experiment. The new wave of apocalypticism, which historians usually call 'premillenialist,' required life to get better before it got worse; that is, there would have to be spiritual improvements, at the very least, to make the world ready for the Second Coming, after which all hell could break out and a final Christian millennium would consummate history. This is what some called 'the doctrine of the rapture, also known as "any-moment" coming,' and it required of the believer a relentlessly high expectation of every moment and a purgatorial discipline of constant self-improvement:

> The new premillenialism placed heavy psychological demands upon believers: enjoined to practice self-purification in anticipation of the final Judgment, they had to consistently hold their intense anticipation in check and turn their attention to organizing their everyday lives by planning for a future that most believed was unlikely at best.[19]

The irony is that some forms of American apocalypticism are an extension of medieval Catholic piety that insisted on self-purification through being born again. After the notion of purgatory became dogma in the late thirteenth century, purgatory soon became a this-worldly state of mind. For hundreds of years Catholic, and then Protestant, piety has sought to develop an acute awareness of the promptings of the divine in everyday life. The believer is to purify the self of every thought and feeling that will not pass muster on the last day, an exercise that, for Catherine of Genoa and her followers, required a second birth. To turn everyday life into a purgatorial discipline directed at self-purification initiated a relentless search for self-development and perfection. Above all, the sense that time itself imposes a discipline on the believer to make the most of every moment and of every day has become an article of secular faith. America became a secular evangelical purgatory that owes as much to John Locke as it does to William Baxter, Catherine of Genoa, Dante, and Augustine.

Among Christians since Augustine there has long been a tendency to secularize the apocalypse and to intensify the significance of the moment. Some have argued that the Last Judgment is a continuing process as Jesus slowly comes into his Kingdom; Christians are already living in the end times. Others believe that the Last Judgment occurred on the cross and that the Second Coming will conclude the period of contest and trial. Because Christians are thus living between the times, every moment may – or may not – put the believer in the divine presence. There are no clear rules for right action, and no guarantees of recognition or reward, although the stakes are high, and the penalties for failure are severe and everlasting. To soften the existential crunch, some believe that even in the present they have an ecstatic connection with the divine, a 'secret rapture,' while others believe that they will someday be initiated into that rapture, as others remain in torment to fight their spiritual battles as best they can. As O'Leary points out, the belief in a secret rapture 'functioned as a mechanism for ethical purification by helping believers to maintain their faith and resist temptation, … [and] gave believers hope that they might avoid not only the catastrophic events of the last days, but also their own personal deaths.' The promise of the rapture makes up for the prospect of a lost future, and in the meantime it gives to each and every moment extraordinary promise and meaning.

Keeping apocalyptic fervor alive, however, requires constant preaching and prophecy. Apocalyptic oratory substitutes the rhetorical moment for the future. It is as if one could magically restore a future that had been lost by dramatizing it and acting it out. That is what O'Leary is getting at when he says of apocalyptic pronouncements that 'the telling of it and the reception of it (whether positive or negative) are proof of it: "And this gospel of the Kingdom will be proclaimed throughout the earth as a testimony to all nations; and then the end will come" (Mt. 24:14).'[20] That is, when the announcement is given, it is as if the future has already begun, so that those who do not believe it have already consigned themselves to outer darkness.

Some apocalyptic preaching tries to convince people that the future that is coming is quite different from one they may have imagined for themselves: everlasting torment instead of consummation, shame instead of honor. The only way to recover the future of which they had dreamed is to renounce their ordinary aspirations and to accept the future that is being offered to them in the fantastic and frightening images of apocalyptic proclamation itself.

> Such purple prose conjures up a picture to satisfy the impatient believer; until the End materializes, its realization in discourse must suffice. William Miller's own recreation of the End completes the scene: 'See, see! the angel with the sharp sickle is about to take the field! See yonder trembling victim fall before his pestilential breath! High and low, rich and poor, trembling and falling before the appalling grave . . .'[21]

When the future you have been longing for no longer seems believable, however, it is as if you have lost your grasp on time itself. It is this experience that is then transposed to the end-time, in the rhetoric of the apocalyptic preacher who warns of a day when the 'living will be struck by the awful cry "There shall be time no longer!" '

By the magic of postponing to the end an experience that has already taken place, the apocalyptic preacher allows you to imagine that your loss of the future is not yet complete; there is still time. All you have to do is to avoid the moment that is the end of all other moments. To do that you must take seriously the possibility that for the faithful 'this dread moment' will arrive, but when it does, another possibility opens up on the darkest of battlefields: 'The clouds have burst asunder; the heavens appear; the great white throne is in sight.'[22] At the very moment when you are facing the end of time, and you have no future at all, the future begins from a source far beyond the stretch of your own imagination. It is as if the preaching of the apocalypse acts out the underlying magical logic of substitution: the replacement of a lost future with a new one.

To accomplish this feat, however, the preacher must simulate the very moments in which people already have experienced a great disappointment: the loss of the only future that they had ever imagined for themselves. When the Greeks were destroying the cities of the Persians in the ancient Middle East, the survivors sought out women in grottoes, the Sybilline oracles, who would tell them of a future that belonged to them. There would come a day when the cities of the enemy would be destroyed, and not their cities only, but the countryside; indeed, not just their countryside, but their ravines. The enemies' whole world would be a smoking ruin. In these pronouncements the new future began, and in that sense these prophecies were self-fulfilling.

Notes

1 Seth Mydans, 'At a School in Russia, a World of Emptiness,' *The New York Times*, September 28, 2004.
2 Stephen O'Leary, *Arguing the Apocalypse: A Theory of Millennial Rhetoric*. New York and Oxford: Oxford University Press, 1994, p. 139.
3 O'Leary, 1994, p. 83.
4 Michel de Montaigne, 'On Sadness,' in *The Complete Essays*, Book 1.2, translated by M.A. Screech. New York and London: Penguin Books, 1987, pp. 7–8.
5 de Montaigne, 'On Sadness,' 1987, p. 8.
6 Ibid.
7 Mansoor Moaddel, 'Ideology as Episodic Discourse: The Case of the Iranian Revolution,' *American Sociological Review*, Vol. 57, Issue 3 (June 1992): 353–379; see esp. pp. 363–5.
8 Nicholas D. Kristof, 'Apocalypse Now?,' *The New York Times*, Book Review Desk, December 12, 1999.
9 Dennis C. Smith, *The Story of the Rescue Efforts at the World Trade Center*, New York: Viking, 2002.
10 Charlie LeDuff, 'Threats and Responses: Deployment; As an American Armada leaves San Diego, Tears are the Rule of the Day,' *New York Times*, Foreign Desk, January 18, 2003.
11 Gershom Gorenberg, *The End of Days: Fundamentalism and the Struggle for the Temple Mount*. New York and London: Oxford University Press, 2000, p. 185.
12 Ibid., pp. 178–80.
13 Ibid., p. 35.
14 Alex Hearn and Peter Klebnikov, 'Apocalypse Now. No. Really, Now,' *New York Times*, 'Magazine Desk,' 27 December 1998.
15 O'Leary, 1994, p. 136, citing Arno Gaebelin, quoted in Timothy Weber, *Living in the Shadow of the Second Coming: American Premillenialism 1875–1982*, revised edition, Chicago: University of Chicago Press, 1987, p. 48.
16 O'Leary, 1994, p. 108.
17 O'Leary, 1994, p. 97.
18 O'Leary, 1994, p. 98.
19 O'Leary, 1994, pp. 136–7.
20 O'Leary, 1994, p. 88.
21 O'Leary, 1994, p. 114, quoting from Froom, *The Prophetic Faith of Our Fathers*, Vol. 4, p. 477.
22 O'Leary, 1994, p. 114, quoting from William Miller, letter to Truman Hendryx, 26 March 1832, reprinted in Sylvester Bliss, *Memoirs of William Miller*, p. 102.

CHAPTER 2

Radical Preachers and Mullahs

Something profound has changed in the capacity of states to control violence. When people now my age were young, we knew that there were two states with a monopoly on nuclear weapons; no longer is that true. We knew that the two states could recognize and negotiate with each other in ways that might avert mutually assured destruction. We knew that brinkmanship was dangerous, but that the players in that game did not believe that 'stuff happens,' or count on Jesus to save them from the Antichrist. Times have changed. In the aftermath of the attack on the World Trade Center in New York City on September 11, 2001, David Runciman, writing in the *London Review of Books*, noted:

> Suddenly, the Hobbesian view that states and states alone have the power and the security to operate under the conditions of lawfulness is threatened by the knowledge that even the most powerful states are vulnerable to assault from unknown and unpredictable sources. It can now be said that in the international arena 'the weakest has strength to kill the strongest,' or they would do, if only they could get their hands on the necessary equipment. It means that international law can no longer be relied on, and that its restraining hand can no longer be expected to control the fearfulness even of those who appear for the outside to have least to fear.
>
> The common view that 11 September 2001 marked the return to a Hobbesian world is therefore entirely wrong. It marked the beginning of a post-Hobbesian age, in which a new kind of insecurity threatens the familiar structures of modern political life ... And since they are not designed to deal with this sort of threat, even the most powerful states don't know what to do about it.[1]

As Runciman pointed out, the state, intrusive and omnipresent though it is, is unable to protect its citizens from its own enemies. No wonder, then, that apocalyptic literature and beliefs resonate powerfully with a wide range of people and have such a highly destructive potential for our times.

The same factors that make the state relatively impotent also make apocalyptic beliefs a clear and present danger not only to national security but to the structures that make everyday life possible. Under

modern conditions, individuals and groups have unprecedented freedom to associate with one another across a wide range of social barriers;
they threaten armed conflict as a way to resolve all outstanding
differences; and they envisage a world of uniformity enforced by sacred
violence. Under these conditions, public spaces, streets, waterways,
networks for communication and travel, for saving, transporting, and
spending money, for exchanging ideas and reaching agreements, for
discovering new medicines, insecticides, and crops: all these modern
connections and innovations provide the matrices in which social life
can flourish. However, they also provide the means by which the few
can terrorize and destroy the many, with or without the aid or
intervention of the state. Modern social systems are indeed like the
Internet. They are constituted by messages flowing through an open
pattern of communication that has no particular center and no
periphery: easily exploited around the clock by terrorists, investment
bankers, subversives, and speculators intent on making a killing. There
is not time for the CIA to find a translator for specific messages that
they cannot decode from moment to moment; immediacy is a matter of
life and death.

Modernity intensifies the hatreds that separate the East from the
West, but it is apocalyptic beliefs that solidify the enmity between the
Islamic and the Christian worlds into passions that are enduring,
intractable, and above all hell-bent on a bloody finale. Until the
Christian churches take the lead in disowning these beliefs, they will
continue to lend the authority of their tradition to those demanding a
final solution to the conflict between Christianity and Islam, East and
West.

The churches must act soon and decisively because the Christian right
has long promoted the notion that these are the times predicted in the
apocalyptic visions of the New Testament, when Israel at long last will
return to the full possession of its land. We all are to be encouraged 'as
we approach the cataclysmic end of the age,' because 'Israel will be
surrounded by her enemies, fighting for her life, and the Lord Himself
will come to defend her' (Robertson 2003: 268). These events will usher
in an age when the survivors of Israel will in turn be converted to
Christianity. Christians are entitled to this triumph. It has been long
predicted, by none other than Jesus himself, and they have waited a very
long time indeed for it to come.

The new world order, modern industry and technology, does cause
unprecedented and irreversible changes in the ways in which people live,
raise children, and make things. Modernity drastically alters the way in
which people work and play. New technology allows people to
communicate with strangers across vast distances, probe the secrets of

the human cell or the distant universe, while enabling the state to keep populations under surveillance and to expose millions to microbes and radiation. Not only do these developments facilitate the integration and effectiveness of terrorist networks; they also make many people feel as if the future is beginning while they are losing their ties with the past and with their local communities. Add a state that is both increasingly intrusive and yet also unable to protect its citizens from danger to the other more generic insults of modernity and you have the conditions that call for a radical transformation of social life. Modernity can begin when a people's defenses crumble and foreigners pour in across the boundaries and through the city gates. In the fifth century invaders introduced Rome to the shock of violent and immediate social change, the modern, as they have the residents of places like Cairo and Baghdad at the turn of the recent millennium.

It is therefore not at all surprising that in the aftermath of the 1967 war Egyptian radicals felt a heightened despair about the vitality of Islamic societies and demanded the radical transformation of these societies into icons of Islamic social order. As Lawrence Wright (2002: 63) put it:

> The speed and the decisiveness of Israel's victory in the Six Day War humiliated Muslims who had believed that God favored their cause. They lost not only their armies and territory but also faith in their leaders, in their countries, and in themselves. For many Muslims, it was as though they had been defeated by a force far larger than the tiny country of Israel, by something unfathomable – modernity itself. A newly strident voice was heard in the mosques, one that answered despair with a simple formulation: Islam is the solution.

It was not only defeat in the Vietnam War but the sudden victory of Islamic terrorists on September 11, 2001 that introduced Americans to the shock of a new, and therefore modern, age. The more feverish the apocalyptic imagination becomes, the more it finds alien influences within American society corrupting individuals in high places. The Jews and the Catholics have now been replaced by secular humanists and homosexuals in the fundamentalists' pantheon of evil influences. Apocalyptic enthusiasts call for a new prophet, a new Elijah, who will reveal the hidden corruption of American society and purify it from inner subversion, and in George Bush many of them feel they have found the man of God's own choosing. Those harboring apocalyptic visions know that evil thrives just beneath the surface of American social life. They see the people of good social standing, the liberal leaders and the apparently upright, as in fact secret unbelievers, adulterers, and sympathizers with the enemy. That is why 'liberals from Massachusetts' are suspect of being not as good as they seem; their honors, like Kerry's medals for service in Vietnam, are unmerited. Like the Antichrist, who is clearly a virtuoso at deception, these people in high places appear to be virtuous and just, but they are wolves in sheep's clothing (Alexander 1985: 194–5). Just as in the Byzantine tradition, the Last Roman Emperor will come in the nick of time to defeat the enemies of justice and orthodoxy, so, too, American apocalypticists call for a savior who will expose the enemies of the people of God, restore devotion to its proper place in public life, and shame the nation's enemies with spectacular defeat (Alexander 1985: 160). No wonder the image-makers portrayed George W. Bush as just such a 'strong leader:' decisive, resolute, consistent, and destined to succeed. Indeed, the apocalypticists long to dissolve outstanding social differences in a purge of every hidden sin.

'Modernity' is just another word for this sense that the pace of history is quickening and that the old order is disintegrating. That is because the modern brings the new and unprecedented, the unique and irreversible, and these always threaten any social order. This sense of final hope in the midst of desperation reflects and intensifies the vast insecurities that accompany modernity. The new is always unsettling, in every age. In modern societies, jobs and capital are like the wind, passing through a place, and then they are gone. Outsourcing not only takes jobs away from local communities, from friends and family, from school teachers and local mechanics, but it also takes capital itself, the life-blood of capitalist societies. With no investment and savings left, the people are being drained of life itself. Thus every individual and community feels threatened and expendable. As individual hopes for recognition and security are dashed, political rhetoric becomes more cynical. Long before old scores are settled in modern societies, new injuries are added. The rich get richer, while old grievances persist. If the Republicans have succeeded in widening the gap between the rich and the poor, they have also succeeded in inflaming the resentments of whites that the unworthy poor, notably black and Hispanic, are not only taking jobs from the whites but also getting government aid, 'welfare handouts.' Not only do the poor whites get poorer and begin to lose their precarious foothold on middle-class status; they add fresh resentment to their old insecurities about their superiority over non-whites. These are some of the conditions conducive to fascism and other forms of political and social reaction. Add to these chronic class, ethnic, racial, and regional animosities the threat of pervasive nuclear terror, and you have a few of the factors that make apocalyptic visions more popular, and also more dangerously self-fulfilling, than ever before.

On the margins of social life, people are often afraid that time is against them. Many of the militias and reactionaries on the far right remember the day on which the federal government, through the FBI and the ATF, decided that time had run out for the Branch Davidians cloistered in their Waco compound, and regardless of who it was that initially opened fire, the result was that the entire community was incinerated. Two years later, to the day, Timothy McVeigh, leveled the federal office building in Oklahoma City in a conscious and quite clear reference to the earlier disaster. The apocalyptic imagination remembers disasters to the day and speeds up the time when that day will be redeemed in another bloodbath. Now, however, apocalypticism is not a fringe movement; with the rise of the Christian right to political prominence, it has moved into the mainstream.

Modernity has always been a word for conditions that make some societies more vulnerable or even moribund. Indeed, as LeGoff notes, 'The word modern comes into being in the fifth century, with the collapse of the Roman empire,' and it connotes 'the feeling of having broken with the past.'[2] As Kermode suggests, the apocalyptic notion of a critical period of transition has been changed into a sense of our times as being 'an age of perpetual crisis in morals and politics. And so, changed by our special pressures, subdued by our skepticism, the paradigms of apocalypse continue to lie under our ways of making sense of the world.'[3]

From a conventional viewpoint, the modern world may have begun with the French Revolution, but that revolution itself was a massive protest against modernity as I am using the word in this argument. Modernity does tear apart traditional communities and widen the gap between the rich and the poor. Modernity also releases a wide range of individual passions that threaten not only the solidarity of traditional communities and of the family but actual livelihoods and lives. That is why so many of the movements are grouped collectively under the heading of the fascist, reactionary rather than revolutionary. Some groups even sound puritanical, or as if they were the forebears of the Christian right. Some of the early Republicans during that revolution were in fact defending family values, denouncing individualism and egoism, greed and self-indulgence. Others were attacking the rich and seeking to close the gap between wealth and desolation. Still others were defending the purity of the revolution itself, so that all those who were not in favor of democracy were enemies of the people and to be driven out or exterminated. The guillotine served the purpose of ridding democracy of the people who

were not deemed fit to live in a democratic society. As Barrington
Moore puts it:

> The behaviors that surfaced in the French Revolution were the
> familiar ones of militant monotheism. There was the usual
> demonization and dehumanization of actual and potential oppo-
> nents. Revolutionaries perceived them as outsiders, threats to
> human society who should be expelled and killed. A substantial
> number, then inhabitants of the Vendee, for instance, were social
> outsiders to begin with. Aristocrats and the well-to-do, against
> whom latent hostility increased to hatred, became 'enemies of the
> people' and thereby demonized by the internal dynamic of the
> Revolution. This process of creating legitimate internal targets
> appears to have been relatively new and especially ominous. In
> earlier persecutions the 'outsiders' were often ready made into what
> Max Weber referred to as 'pariah peoples,' Jews and Kurds, or
> Canaanites and Philistines, competitors for the same land. That
> one's own society could secrete moral pollution seems to have been
> a new idea, at least in terms of the degree of emphasis it received.[4]

There is more than irony in Moore's argument that the revolutionaries
were reactionaries or that what appeared to be a secular movement
harbored the old totalitarian, authoritarian, and exclusivist impulses of
monotheistic religion. There is also a warning here for those who are
baffled by the radicalism of the republican movements in the USA in the
early twenty-first century. The democratic vision of the president,
George W. Bush, that inspires him to lead a crusade on Middle Eastern
soil to liberate people from oppression, or to install women as equal
partners of men in the body politic of Afghanistan, or to imagine a
fraternity of democratic nations linking the West to the Islamic world, is
notably associated with unprecedented increases in the power of the
state to repress domestic dissent and disagreement with his policies.
Those who criticize the war are aiding and abetting the enemy while
undermining the morale of the troops. Those who critique the
government find out that they have been put on a list of people to be
carefully watched, perhaps when they discover that the airlines will not
issue them a ticket. Citizens of the wrong descent are deprived of their
civil liberties and incarcerated without access to the judicial process. The
Republican administration is thus not the first to imagine a system in
which people are allowed to move about if they have an internal
passport, while others find their freedom of movement radically
restricted. Granted that the Department of Homeland Security has
yet to adopt the more draconian methods of the revolutionaries'
Committee of Public Safety, the revolutionary impulse is clear: to

protect the people from the enemies of democracy even if that means an assault on their privacies and liberties.

The radicalism of the current regime is thus based on the apocalyptic and moral enthusiasms of the Christian right, although in its policy formulations it is the secularized religion of democracy that is being used to provide ideological cover for expansionism and intervention. Furthermore, in their domestic policies, the current batch of Republicans share with their French antecedents an enthusiasm for self-discipline, constraints on sexual morality and the expression of individual freedoms, and a strong conviction of the moral benefits of hard work. As Barrington Moore puts it of the French revolutionary Saint-Just:

> Corrupt morals he contrasted with a conscious and willing acceptance of obligations to society together with contentment in hard work, sexual restraint, and the idealized set of what today might be called 'family values'. All this was pure. Except perhaps for the emphasis on social obligations, it is hard to discern anything in Saint-Just's distinction between pure and corrupt morals that would fail to receive enthusiastic endorsement from the most reactionary United States senator or leader of the Christian Right, as well as a large number of less controversial figures. Thus the most radical and 'pure' goals of the French Revolution became in two centuries the mental baggage of Western reactionaries.

There are important differences in the extent to which various groups or classes in modern societies can cope with change, defeat, and disaster. Some in the middle classes have been able to make a fetish of the modern. In a sense, they have come to idolize the new and to elevate the fleeting and transitory into something eternal. James Moorhead (2002: 87ff.) has recounted how the more frightening and disruptive visions of the Kingdom of God in Christian apocalyptic were softened by the end of the last century by being fused with images of social progress and individual perfection: 'The preoccupation with natural growth, the denial of limits (especially death), the desire for open-ended movement, and the fear of stasis were rooted in major cultural and intellectual transformations. The triumph of a consumerist ethos offered interesting parallels with the new eschatology' (Moorhead 2002: 93). Thus the Kingdom of God would come continually; its advent would itself be a process rather than an event. The coming of the Kingdom was therefore coterminous with the continuing extension of a democratic polity and capitalist economy, with consumption replacing sacrifice and the voice of the people replacing the cries of the penitent. For many of the

Protestants Moorhead is describing, death itself was reduced to something like a hiccup after a good meal and a prelude to further, happy digestion of life's accomplishments and remaining desires.[5] That is why the middle class is so important in the politics of modern and modernizing nations. They are the ones who have a taste for incremental change and the capacity to bring it about. They also have the most to lose in any collapse of the market, since they depend on income from jobs rather than on assets that can be transported from one nation to another, and they have lost their precarious possession of the land. No wonder that John Kerry, in the 2004 presidential campaign in the USA, saw the importance of stability in the middle class as a necessary antidote to the politics of resentment and apocalypticism. Only among those whose lives are less circumscribed by sickness, migration, poverty, and violence does the future seem achievable through the processes of slow and careful change rather than through the drastic remedies of national self-purification.

However, many even of those who are comfortable with the uncertainties and losses of life in modern societies turn to the comforts and assurances offered by apocalyptic beliefs. Because apocalypticism offers self-fulfilling prophecies of disaster, it is all the more imperative for the churches to discredit their own apocalyptic traditions and to call upon the USA to abandon its claims to supremacy and triumph. Otherwise the nation must endure the most vicious civil conflict, and in the international arena it will be headed for Armageddon.

In acting as though it has no limits in space or time, the USA fills the world with fear and hatred, and it breeds new generations of those who long for vengeance. This is collective madness, and much of it has been fed and sustained by Christian apocalyptic literature and popular belief in a Day of Judgment. So long as the churches continue to hold sacred their own apocalyptic beliefs, however, they are in no position to look down on the apocalyptic enthusiasts of the 'Christian' right, who think of the USA as the new Israel headed for triumph in the final battle against evil.

Islamic Apocalypticism

I am arguing that modernity, and a state that is both weaker and yet more intrusive, make people feel unsure about the survival of their communities and ways of life. Outside influences seem more dangerous and pervasive; internal sources of disbelief and change seem more threatening. Trust in institutions and leaders declines, and a sense that the state in particular is dangerous, especially when in the hands of unbelievers, creates a demand for social transformation and purity in politics. The more a community seems to be vulnerable, and the more the state seems to be ineffective in protecting the society against outside influences, the more the apocalyptic imagination finds support in the fantasies and despair of the people themselves.

Take, for example, this story from *The New York Times* of October 12, 2004, 'God Has 4,000 Loudspeakers: The State Holds Its Ears,' by Neil MacFarquhar:

CAIRO – Given the cacophony that afflicts any Cairo street – the braying donkeys, the caterwauling vegetable vendors, the constant honking of car horns – it might seem a particularly daunting task to single out just one noise to prosecute as the most offensive.

But the minister of religious endowments recently did that, more or less, making a somewhat unlikely decision in these times when many Muslim faithful believe that their religion is under assault.

The call to prayer, the minister declared, is out of control: too loud, too grating, utterly lacking in beauty or uniform timing, and hence in dire need of reform. The solution, the evidently fearless minister decided – harking back to an answer Egyptian bureaucrats have seized upon since long before Islam – is to centralize it.

The minister, Mahmoud Hamdi Zaqzouq, announced that one official call to prayer would be broadcast live from one central Cairo mosque five times a day, and that it would be carried simultaneously by the 4,000-plus mosques and prayer halls across the capital.

From the ensuing national brouhaha – the outraged headlines, the scathing editorials, the heated debates among worshipers – one might gain the impression that Mr. Zaqzouq was leading an assault against Islam itself. 'Minarets Weep,' intoned one banner headline, while another suggested sarcastically that the minister was less than a good Muslim. 'The Call to Prayer Upsets Minister,' it read.

Comedians and intellectuals had a field day. Ali Salem, one of Egypt's leading playwrights, envisioned a turbaned, high-tech SWAT team dispatched across Cairo whenever one mosque or another inevitably sabotaged the centralized prayer-call operation.

Not everyone ridiculed the idea, though.

Secular Cairenes endorsed it as a possible means toward greater government control over all of the tiny storefront mosques that have often proved a font of violent, extremist Islam. And Mr. Zaqzouq insisted that his proposal enjoyed wide grass-roots popularity.

In the surging religious environment of the last decade, the multiplication of mosques and prayer halls is such that any random Cairo street might house half a dozen, each competing with the others in volume and staggering the timing of their call slightly in an effort to stand out.

Particularly at dawn prayers, some mosques blast not just the roughly dozen sentences of the call itself, but all of the Koranic verses and actual prayers intoned by the local imam. When three different mosques do the same thing, what should be an announcement lasting at most two minutes can drag on for 45 minutes, keeping the entire neighborhood awake.

'There are loudspeakers that shake the world,' the minister protested. 'Everyone hears them. Every day I receive bitter complaints from people about the loudspeakers, but when I ask them to register official complaints, they say they fear others will accuse them of being infidels.'

Opponents, meanwhile, express deep outrage at the very idea of someone tampering with the tradition of each mosque having its own muezzin, of different voices echoing across the city in a continuous round.

'During the time of the Prophet there used to be more than one mosque in each town, in each quarter, and he didn't unify the prayer, so why do it now?' asked Sheik Mustafa Ali Suliman, who works as a muezzin in a small mosque amid the twisting streets of Cairo's medieval quarter. 'There is even a saying by the Prophet Muhammad that implies that in God's eyes muezzins will garner special honor and respect on judgment day.'

Given the widespread sentiment that no decent Muslim could ever consider such a change, no small number of Cairo residents seized on the obvious alternative: it is a C.I.A. plot, they muttered, right up there with other American attacks on Islam, like demanding changes in the Muslim world's curriculums.

The conspiracy theorists further prophesied that the centralized system was just a test case for the real goal: to disseminate a single Friday Prayer sermon, written, naturally, in Langley, Va. The outcry reached such a level that the minister felt obliged to hold an hour-long news conference to quell the sense, as he put it, that doomsday was at hand.

The instructions did not, in fact, come from Washington, he said. 'Opponents call this initiative an American one, as if every step of reform should come through instructions from abroad,' Mr. Zaqzouq said dismissively.

The most serious religious charge against him was that centralizing the call to prayer would amount to 'bida,' an innovation bordering on heresy. While Saudi Arabia's Wahhabi clergymen tend to be the all-star team of bida police, slapping the label on practices like giving flowers to hospital patients or using mobile phones with cameras, declaring something bida in Egypt is far less common.

The minister was having none of it.

'The real bida is the loudspeaker,' Mr. Zaqzouq said. 'Islam did just fine without loudspeakers for 1,350 years.' Any mosque where the muezzin wants to climb up into the minaret and sing out the call to prayer without electronic amplification will be exempt from the centralized system, he promised.

There were also dire predictions that the change would throw at least 100,000 muezzins out of work in a country already suffering severe unemployment. The minister said that the proposal was just for Cairo, although the country's other 26 governorates could follow suit if they wanted, and that the capital had exactly 827 officially recognized muezzins, who could surely find other useful tasks around each mosque.

Various clerics said they hoped the proposal would remain 'under study' for years to come, and indeed Mr. Salem, the playwright, unearthed a joke predating the automobile that he said underscored the timeless nature of the debate.

A Maltese visitor riding a donkey through an Egyptian village hears what he considers beautiful music and asks his dragoman the source. 'That is our call to prayer, sir,' the guide responds, and the Maltese adopts the Muslim faith on the spot.

By the next prayer time, a few hours later, they have arrived at a different village, where the muezzin calls out with a particularly ugly, rasping voice. 'Hurry up, hurry up,' the dragoman says, beating the donkey to speed it through the village, 'lest our visitor hear the muezzin and recant.'

In the compass of one small story, the writer has noted how small communities and neighborhoods, centered in a local religious institution, seem to be threatened by a state that intrudes on them even while being a vehicle for foreign influences. The community may lose control over its way of life, and at least the local clergy may be out of a job. The demands for centralized control, the force of the state, and yet its inability to shelter and preserve local communities and livelihoods: these are the core ingredients of the threats posed by social change and modernity not only to the people of Cairo, Egypt, but of Cairo, Illinois. No wonder there were dire predictions and doomsday scenarios, as the Cairenes felt they were running out of time and demanded both rescue and a final judgment of their cause.

Apocalyptic beliefs articulate precisely such a demand in pronouncements of a coming Day of Judgment. Take, for example, Ayman al-Zawahiri, now the number two leader of Al Qaeda, hiding perhaps in the hills between Pakistan and Afghanistan, who was born in 1951 to an elegant and accomplished Egyptian family that had numbered among its members at least two presidents of Egypt's major universities. In order to protest the domination of the town by a Westernized Egyptian elite, his family chose to live on the wrong side of the tracks, where he developed the viewpoint of the oppressed and humiliated Egyptian: Islam had been outclassed by the West and, in the war of 1967, outgunned by Israel. Deeply religious and reactionary, he wished to see Egypt revitalized under clerical rule and subject to Islamic law, as if such measures would enable the Islamic world finally to turn the tables on 'the empire of the United States and the world's Jewish government.'[6] Like the apocalyptic visionaries of the Christian right in the United States, who look forward to Israel's control of all the promised land and to a final Armageddon, Zawahiri similarly looks forward to the destruction of Israel and the world dominance of Islam. Like the Moral Majority and Christian Coalition in the United States, Zawahiri fears a new world order, despises secular government, and trusts that Israel's effort will fail.

For those who see such defeats in apocalyptic terms, the future can only bring a cataclysmic and final encounter with the forces of evil. That is because the apocalyptic imagination demands a final test of will and strength. In the Byzantine tradition, a Last Roman Emperor will finally defeat the enemies of the people of God in apocalyptic battle.[7] On his triumphal return, the Last Roman Emperor will conquer and exterminate the infidels, Arabs and Turks or other Ishmaelites, the forces of Gog and Magog, and even the Jews (Alexander 1985: 163–6). Indeed, the Last Emperor will 'come as the final executor of God's judgment and His proof over His creation' (Ayoub 1978: 198). The final battle, however, can only be won by divine assistance, and in it many will perish in a collective exorcism of all forms of difference. Furthermore, the triumph of the people of God over their enemies must be paid for in advance by various forms of collective self-immolation: defeat, tribulation, humiliation, and despair. Even the Last Roman Emperor typically waits in the wings while the enemy taunts the Christians by claiming that the Christians lack any savior (Alexander 1985: 154). Only when it appears that the Arabs, who have won many battles, will apparently vanquish the Christian world will the Last Roman Emperor arrive to eliminate the enemies of the people of God. In the end, even he will surrender his crown to God after his final victory: an act, I would argue, of consummate self-immolation (Alexander 1985: 151, 162–5).

If Christians respond to defeats, to globalization, and to modernity with apocalyptic beliefs and visions, so do Muslims. Islam has long entertained dreams of a hero returning at the end of time to judge the world and to vindicate his faithful followers. Indeed, as the Islamic group the Ithna 'Ashari Shi'a continue to believe, the twelfth and final

Imam will return as the eternal Mahdi.[8] On that day, there will indeed be 'absolute vengeance' (Ayoub 1978: 198). All those loyal followers who have shared in the sufferings of the imams join with the imams themselves in the final 'acts of redemption, healing, and judgment' (Ayoub 1978: 198).

During the Islamic revolution in Iran, Ayatollah Khomeini's supporters claimed him to be the manifestation of the long-awaited and long-hidden Imam whose coming, at the end, would signify that the time for Islam's world triumph was at hand. Preaching martyrdom as the only way to salvation, Khomeini gave hundreds of thousands of young people the chance to die for the faith in the war with Iraq. For years now, the more sectarian and extreme among Islamic clerics have been promoting a particularly hateful form of Islamic apocalyptic belief that the time is coming for an ultimate showdown with the infidels, the enemies of Islam.[9] Particularly Israel and its friends, Britain and the United States, are believed to be due for devastating defeats at the hands of Islam. Prompted by the humiliating failure of Arab countries to defeat Israel in the 1967 war, some Islamic clerics have breathed new life into ancient dreams of Islamic glory. No one should doubt that, when the Ayatollahs of Iran speak of the United States as the 'Great Satan,' they are signaling the beginning of the end for the enemies of Islam. The sign of that beginning was the emergence of Ayatollah Khomeini himself as Imam: the first use of that title by any leader since the end of the ninth century (Amanat 2000: 256). The glorious days of the past will come again, as the Islamic revolution deals a death blow to Israel and the United States.

The sufferings of the imams and their followers will therefore prove to have been the prologue to final victory and revenge. Muslims indeed hope for a final day in which all accounts will be settled, and the Islamic faith will at last be supreme. Thus Sayyid Qutb writes from an Egyptian prison in the 1950s: 'Mankind today is on the brink of a precipice. Humanity is threatened not only by nuclear annihilation but by the absence of values. The West has lost its vitality, and Marxism has failed. At this crucial and bewildering juncture, the turn of Islam and the Muslim community has arrived.'[10] As for Christianity, Qutb (1993: 16ff.) writes, it was hopelessly compromised from the outset by the complicated myths and beliefs that it adopted under the influence of Roman civilization.

According to Lawrence Wright (2002: 62), stories about Sayyid Qutb's sufferings in prison, his torture and humiliation at the hands of the prison officials, became a sort of 'Passion play for Islamic fundamentalists.' In his sufferings Muslims in many countries could see a parable of their own humiliation, not only at the hands of the West but by their own governments, which were becoming increasingly Westernized and thus indifferent or hostile to the virtues and convictions of the people. Qutb praised the ability of Islam to get along with other faiths, but he also claimed that universal peace depends on the world adopting Islamic principles.[11] These alone provide a framework for justice, equality, and liberation for the oppressed, because 'Islamic social justice is more comprehensive and more complete when compared to other social doctrines' (Qutb 1993: 3). The Muslim, therefore, is to fight against all those who prevent free choice of religion, but the free choice Qutb has in mind is the willingness either to convert to Islam or to pay tribute for the sake of receiving protection from an Islamic country (Qutb 1993: 10). There will be a Last Day, and only those who have made their peace with Islam will be spared the everlasting fire.

As Ayoub (1978: 199) argues, 'imamology is a kind of Islamic Christology.' Thus the Christian churches are in no position to make improving speeches either to Islamic or Christian extremists so long as the churches believe that Jesus Christ will come again on the Last Day to throw the faithless and the wicked into everlasting hell, while redeeming his own from such torments and ushering them into eternal blessedness. Such beliefs simply vindicate an Islamic tradition that longs for the devastation of all those whom it regards as unbelievers.

Of course, it would be a mistake to characterize all Muslims as carriers of an apocalyptic tradition that is as militant and brutal in its visions of Islam's triumph as are the extremist versions of apocalyptic belief among the millions of American Protestants who subscribe to views like those of Pat Robertson. Among Muslims there are many who do see the hour of final conflict and judgment in the quite literal terms offered by the Koran: a temporary, purifying purgatorial fire for deserving Muslims, but for Christians and Jews, idolaters and hypocrites, a fire that will be far more excruciating and lasting (Smith and Haddad 2002: 85).

However, there are other Muslims who, like Christian modernists, tend to see Hell and Heaven in terms that are far more spiritual than physical, more symbolic than literal, more personal than collective in their judgments. For these Islamic modernizers, then, there is a chance for continuous progress toward Heaven, beginning in this life and continued in the next; even in Heaven itself there may be continuing discoveries as the saved contemplate new horizons in their visions of God (Smith and Haddad 2002: 133ff.). The modernizers, Islamic and Christian alike, tend to secularize their own traditions, in the sense that permanent states of being are reduced to temporary ones, so that progress can affect the soul and thus the fate of the believer in this life and in the next: so much so that for some Islamic authorities even Hell is temporary, at least for the Muslims. Progress, however, is for the faithful and not the infidel. Thus, there are some highly influential Islamic authorities who still believe that 'while those who have embraced the true religion of God [Islam-rkf] will be delivered from the Fire after expiation, even if they are guilty of atrocious crimes, the infidels will be doomed to eternal damnation' (Smith and Haddad 2002: 143). The line is still drawn when it comes to those who are not followers of the true religion: for them Hell is for ever.

My point is not that there is theological intransigence even among progressive Islamic scholars and religious authorities. That may be true, but I am not an Islamicist, and it is far beyond the scope of my own competence to venture a guess as to what aspects of current Islamic thought are popular, let alone authoritative or likely to be considered orthodox in various parts of the Islamic world. I suspect that there are as many differences among Muslims as there are between Muslims and Christians on how to imagine the end of the world and the possibilities of a salvation for all, regardless of their secular condition or their religious community.

Thus although apocalyptic beliefs purport to envisage the future, they simply recode past cataclysms into a scenario of eventual destruction. Instead then of a clash of civilizations between Islam and Christianity or Judaism, we have a dispute between sectarian wings of a common, apocalyptic civilization. Islam still embodies apocalyptic visions of the future. In Shi-ite belief, the once and future Imam, 'the Lord of Time,' will return to do battle against 'the false Messiah,' and there will be 'the raising of the dead on the Plane of the Gathering, the Final Judgment, the Heaven's bliss, and the torments of Hell.'[12] Indeed, even as the American colonists were bracing themselves for cosmic battles against unbelievers and the Antichrist, against the forces of Satan and of the indigenous American Indian peoples, Shi-ite theology in Persia and the East was stirring up 'a mass of millennial yearning often with revolutionary potentials' against both institutionalized religion and the state (Amanat 2000: 239).

Not all Persian apocalyptic movements have been so militant. For cataclysmic events, some have substituted a purgatorial process of continuing self-perfection and have drawn heavily on Hellenistic thought concerning the progress of the soul. However, modernity and the colonial experience have intensified apocalyptic yearnings in Islam, as they also have in Western Christianity. It is therefore impossible to distinguish modern Islam from Christianity as though one is wholly Eastern and the other from the West. Both are developments, however antagonistic, within a common civilization.

The last two centuries have seen a number of movements seeking to revitalize Islam through the sacrifice of true believers martyred by their own faithless, corrupt, and Westernized governments (Amanat 2000: 241ff.). Certainly, what Islamic leaders had in mind when they sent young people to their death on the Iraqi front was a sort of collective exorcism: a violent cleansing. In its aftermath, the dead would immediately enjoy the pleasures of paradise, while the living would be able to enjoy a world purified of the enemies of God. Cries of 'Death to America' had then, as they have now, the effect of a magic formula for exorcizing an evil demon. Thus those seeking to be more progressive and to bring the blessings of science and democracy to the people have kept the apocalyptic faith. Even the more peaceful and utopian movements still required a break with the past and looked forward to a violent, collective upheaval in order to introduce a new future of purity as well as progress (Amanat 2000: 243–4). That is just the point. Even Islam's progressives and rationalists have not said, once and for all, that the time has come to abandon the apocalyptic framework of their faith. The mass of Muslims continue to believe in a day when the Lord will return, and while the faithful will be judged along with everyone else, they will be spared the final torments and Hell itself, Heaven being their eternal reward (Amanat 2000: 248ff.). The apocalyptic climate in Islam, as on the Christian right, nourishes the current crop of radicals spoiling for a fight.

Notes

1 David Runciman, 'A Bear Armed with a Gun,' *London Review of Books*, Vol. 25, Number 7, 3 April 2003, p. 5.
2 Jacques LeGoff, *History and Memory*, translated by Steven Rendall and Elizabeth Claman. New York: Columbia University Press, 1992, p. 23.
3 Frank Kermode; *The Sense of an Ending: Studies in the Theory of Fiction with a New Epilogue*. New York and Oxford: Oxford University Press, 2000, p. 28.
4 Barrington Moore, Jr, *Moral Purity and Persecution in History*. Princeton, NJ: Princeton University Press, 2000, p. 103.
5 Of course, this account of modernity draws far more heavily on upper-middle-class Protestant theology than on the long memories of African-Americans, burdened still by the memory of terror and humiliation and by the recurring experience of exclusion and sudden death at the hands of white mobs. It is an account that does not focus on the recurrent revivals of piety among Catholics in the USA and on their continued devotion to the dead through prayer and sacrifice.
6 Ayman al-Zawahiri, no title, no date; quoted in Lawrence Wright, 'The Man Behind Bin Laden,' *The New Yorker*, September 16, 2002, p. 63.
7 Paul J. Alexander, *The Byzantine Apocalyptic Tradition*. Berkeley and Los Angeles: University of California Press, 1985, p. 151ff.

8   Karen Isaksen Leonard, *Muslims in the United States: The State of Research*. New York: Russell Sage Foundation, 2003, pp. 35–6.
9   In this discussion I am following closely the argument of Abbas Amanat, 'The Resurgence of Apocalyptic in Modern Islam,' in *The Encyclopedia of Apocalypticism*, Vol. 3, *Apocalypticism in the Modern Period and the Contemporary Age*, edited by Stephen J. Stein. New York: Continuum Publishing, 2000, pp. 230–64.
10 From 'Ma'alim fi al-Tariq,' quoted in Lawrence Wright, 'The Man Behind Bin Laden,' *The New Yorker*, September 16, 2002, p. 62.
11 Sayyid Qutb, *Islam and Universal Peace*, Plainfield, Indiana: American Trust Publications, 1993.
12 Abbas Amanat, 'The Resurgence of Apocalyptic in Modern Islam,' in *The Encyclopedia of Apocalypticism*, Vol. 3, *Apocalypticism in the Modern Period and the Contemporary Age*, edited by Stephen J. Stein. New York: Continuum Publishing, 2000: 230–64; pp. 237, 239.

CHAPTER 3

Terror and the Apocalyptic Imagination

The convergence of Judaism, Islam, and Christianity toward an apocalyptic confrontation is both a product of the violence of the twentieth century and a very likely source of cataclysm in the twenty-first. It is all the more important, therefore, to believe with Madison that reason would eventually prevail if religion were allowed to assert itself in the public sphere. If reason is to prevail, however, it will take more than criticisms of apocalyptic enthusiasms among evangelical Protestants and Islamic extremists. The judgments of reason need first to be directed against what might seem to some to be an unlikely target: the mainstream churches, both Protestant and Catholic, that also harbor these beliefs.

Of course, among the mainstream Protestants, there is a long history of moderating apocalyptic beliefs with reason in order to deprive them of some of their more sinister aspects. Some focus on the promise that in the end all tears will be wiped away, and in so doing they say very little about the context of these promises. That context is a vision of end-times in which old grievances are given bloody satisfaction, and the righteous will be comforted by the sight of the suffering of the wicked. Others focus on the possibility that the apocalypse was begun during the life of Jesus Christ, and that everyone since then has been living in a process like the Last Judgment, in which every soul is being continuously held to higher levels of accountability than ever before. Among the reformed Protestant churches in fact, there is a continuing discussion as to whether the Second Coming is a continuing process, an event that will precede the awful trials of the last days, or a stage in history that will arrive when the world has been sufficiently evangelized and societies have been sufficiently Christianized by the work of the Church. Similarly, many Protestants would concur that there is progress toward eternity in this life as well as in the next, and that it is therefore reasonable to think of Hell and Heaven as states of one's being or aspects of the heart and soul, rather than as decisive events that will take place toward the end of history when the dead are resurrected long enough to stand their final trial.

Clearly, the leaders of the Presbyterian Church are not alone among Protestants in wishing to engage Christians in vigorous 'struggle … as if it were the eve of the Last Day, yet without the despair, the haste, and the militancy that accompany the conviction that world history has played out its predestined course and the Day is actually at hand.'[1] Unfortunately, this progressive, pragmatic, and existentialist view of the ultimate significance of everyday life is not all that mainstream Protestants believe. Orthodox Protestants share with Pat Robertson and the millions of fundamentalist or evangelical Christians the belief that, when the Day comes, there will be little hope for non-Christians and even for those who mistakenly call themselves Christians. Mainstream Protestants may be more receptive to metaphors and to secular humanists, not to mention Muslims and homosexuals. They still believe, however, that in the end there will be only two kinds of people: the saved and the unsaved.

Notably, like the Islamic leaders who believe that the fires of Hell can be abated only for Muslims, but for Jews and Christians these flames will blaze eternally, the authors of the Presbyterians' message about the end want to make it clear that 'Humans are saved only in Christ, by grace through faith.'[2] So much for those who have followed the wrong revelation. Toward the Protestants who believe in a Rapture that will separate most of the Christian sheep from all of the goats, followed by tribulations that will complete the process of culling the flock, the Presbyterian document has little patience. This notion of a new dispensation undermines the old covenant, which should be understood to be remaining in full force. As the Presbyterian document concludes, there are important 'boundaries which must be preserved. There is but one overarching covenant of grace, one covenant people, one salvation, one return of Christ, one general resurrection and one Last Judgment.'[3] These are affirmations that can be found in the Presbyterians' Westminister Confession of Faith. That is, they are as authoritative as they are exclusive in their vision of who and what will make the final cut of history. I am arguing for a new dispensation in which there is not only no Jew or Greek, male or female, slave or free, but also no Muslim or Christian, fundamentalist or secular humanist.

These beliefs provide theological cover for the conservatives who carry these convictions out in an American foreign policy that favors the unfettered, unilateral, and pre-emptive exercise of national sovereignty. However, these same beliefs inform the vastly popular series of apocalyptic novels, the *Left Behind* series. The authors of the Presbyterian document castigate the viewpoint of the authors of the novels, Tim La Haye and Jerry Jenkins, because it is theologically unorthodox: there being no warrant in Scripture for a new dispensation but only for 'one Covenant of Grace.'[4] Nonetheless, Presbyterians and fundamentalist extremists share the view that many so-called Christians will suffer, along with the damned, one ghastly consequence after another. Like the modern Islamic scholar Sayyid Qutb, they are willing to see the eschatological hope in terms of psychological states or of moral progress, and they even understand the biblical witness as employing literary figures of speech rather than literal representations (Smith and Haddad 2002: 109,138–9). However, for both Qutb and the Presbyterians, there is only one way to salvation. Even if the mainstream Protestant churches have tended to argue that the apocalypse is either a very long way off, or that it began a long time ago at the crucifixion of Jesus Christ, or that it is a continuing process in the hearts of the faithful, these churches still keep the apocalypse itself as an item of firm belief. Not only will the day come, bringing unprecedented agony as well as joy, but some, who have parted company with Jesus Christ, have already chosen 'the death which is the separation from God.'[5] To sentence non-believers to death is, after all, what orthodox apocalypticism intends.

The convergence of three world religions in their apocalyptic visions is alarming enough when it occurs only among the extremists: the Pat Robertsons among Christians, or the more radical apocalyptic ideologues among the Islamic communities. It is they who promote the hatred and raise hopes for a day on which all scores will be finally settled. It is all the more alarming, however, in view of the fact that the moderate theological communities, the so-called 'mainstream' Protestant churches, also harbor a hard-core apocalypticism: an orthodox commitment to a final solution in which all those who want to be saved will have to recognize the Lordship of Christ. Mainstream Protestantism thus divide the world into two halves: the winners and the losers. Only those will stand the test of time who accept the Christian message and take part in that 'one covenant.' Others, outside the covenant, will have no legs on which to stand before the final tribunal. Conversely, only those will stand the test of time who become Muslims or at least who pay tribute to Islamic sovereignty. In the end, there will be no differences except those authorized by the sovereign religious community.

As I have suggested, some will think it unfair to hold moderate churches to account for the political consequences of apocalyptic beliefs because, for many of their members, these beliefs simply have a metaphoric or existential meaning. It is precisely because these stories are metaphoric, however, that they have such a continuing power from one generation or century to the next. The images of the Book of Revelation, for instance, do refer to the circumstances of the early

Christian community. They do refer to the enmity of the Christians against Rome and to their dreams of eternal glory. However, the images enjoy a certain freedom from their original context. Like the Book of Revelation itself, they point the reader or listener toward a new future opening up in the present.[6] There is something perennially true in the stories of the Book of Revelation, and indeed in all apocalyptic visions: something that is coming true even as the stories themselves are being told and retold. That is why the Christian right can so effectively point these images toward whatever time and place they choose to consider as the scene of the next confrontation between good and evil, Christ and Antichrist, God and Satan. The sophisticated and liberal interpreters of apocalyptic imagery therefore have more in common with the supposedly literal-minded enthusiasts spoiling for Armageddon in their own time than they might wish to acknowledge. They differ only in their sense of how close they are to the end of the story.

Thus apocalyptic visions, Christian or otherwise, have lethal implications in every generation precisely because of their ability to be freely associated with any actual or imagined set of circumstances in the near or relatively distant future. At the same time, however, these visions imagine a world in which freedom of association is strictly limited. The gates of the new Jerusalem may be wide open, but they will admit only the faithful. The only people allowed into the city at the end of time will be those ordained to be there: the Kingdom in which everyone is pure enough to be a priest of God. For true believers, the apocalypse offers a world in which time will go on for ever; their story will never end but will continue to be told and heard, sung and said, for time immemorial.[7] It is only for those who fail to make the final cut of history that the story will come to a brutal and final close, never to be told or repeated.

Until and unless Christians renounce their apocalyptic beliefs, there will be no reason to expect Islamic extremists to be any less insistent in their demands for a final showdown with the West. Of course, the mainstream churches typically deplore collective violence, and, because of their publicly stated cautions against a war in Iraq, they may not understand why anyone would hold them accountable for such violence. How, therefore, could the churches, not those on the Christian right that are spoiling for Armageddon but the more pacific mainstream Protestant denominations and the Catholic Church, be held accountable for a war against 'the axis of evil'? Is it not nationalist passions, rather than Christian apocalypticism, that foments a war on foreign soil against a country that has not attacked America?

Like the mainstream Protestant churches, Catholics also believe that their Lord will return and initiate a final judgment in which the wicked will be sent to the torments of Hell, while the good, the just, and the faithful will inherit everlasting peace and joy. It is a doctrine that has comforted many who long for a day when the wicked get their just deserts, while their own tears will at last be wiped away. Christian churches of whatever persuasion read Scriptures in which their own Lord warns them against the coming of such a day and promises that those who fail the test of time will in fact be thrown into outer darkness and eternal torment. The point, however, is quite simple: that despite all the twisting and turning of theological inference and interpretation, the poisonous doctrine of an apocalyptic day of awful reckoning is kept on the books, in the canon, in the creed, and on the minds, if not always in the hearts, of the faithful. As a friend of mine, a man who has served the USA, at great cost to himself, in the military and who now serves in its churches and prisons, has put it, the churches use apocalyptic imagery to keep alive the virus of hatred because they never know when they might need it. It therefore does not matter if the churches also warn against a literal reading of the Scriptures. Some have suggested that the Last Judgment occurred on the cross, so that we all have been living in the end-times ever since. Others have suggested that the Second Coming is a continuous process in which every time and place is fraught with existential significance. Still the apocalyptic virus remains, ready to infect the body politic with the passion to eliminate all differences and to have the global field to itself.

Conditions under which Apocalypticism Flourishes

The apocalyptic convergence of Islam, Judaism, and Christianity politicizes all belief and practice. It terminates a social contract that allowed religion free reign in society so long as belief and practice were either private or, if they went public, were of no radical consequence for the society as a whole. Apocalypticism politicizes everyday life, in which individuals decide whom to love, how to live, whom to support, how to educate their own and others' children, how medicine should be practiced and who has a right to reasonably good health, what constitutes good science or legitimate art. They have not been politicized simply because the Christian right, for instance, has opinions on so many different subjects. They have not been politicized simply because the state has extended itself into so many nooks and crannies of social and personal life. What constituted privacy, and who may have a right to it, is now a very controversial political issue precisely because an apocalyptic world view has raised the stakes and increased the risks in every aspect of social life. Nothing is merely a temporal matter when the end of time is near.

It has long been understood that, in the USA, religion has been able to resist any attempts to keep it on the margins of social and political life. That success has been due in part to the central role of the mainstream Protestant churches in forming social organizations, shaping communities, and giving legitimacy to the nation-state. It has also been due in part to a constitution that prevents the state from inhibiting the public expression of religious beliefs and sentiments. The right of individuals to free association has extended to the right of communities to publicize their religious beliefs and to inject their concerns into politics. The separation of church from state, not in itself a constitutional principle but a tenet of Jeffersonian democracy, is offset by the free play of religion in the political system: a freedom of association enhanced in part by a constitutional prohibition against requiring individuals to pass a particular religious test in order to hold office. Structural barriers have allowed religion itself to inform, protest, and to legitimate the political arrangements of the national community. In that sense, there is nothing new in the current influence of religious communities on social policy.

I do not mean to underestimate the importance of the state's expansion. Talal Asad (2003: 199) pointed out is the extent to which the state itself has a warrant to extend itself into every aspect of social and personal life. Thus the state even defines what constitutes privacy. Furthermore, as societies in which Islam is dominant in the population have become increasingly exposed to Western influences, they have become increasingly concerned with the formation and expansion of the state. That is why it is unfair, Asad (2003: 199) argues, to blame Muslims for being nationalistic or anti-democratic when they wish to live under a state that supports Islamic principles; Islam itself has had to become increasingly 'statist' simply to survive in a global field dominated by other states.

However, it is apocalypticism that enables the state to demand a final solution. From the fall of Troy to the destruction of Jerusalem, from the fall of Rome in the sixth century to the civil wars that repeatedly devastated Europe and the USA, from the Crusades to the genocides caused by the European invasion of the 'new world,' apocalyptic beliefs have promised a return engagement, a final turning of the tables. Those promises are a luxury that the world can no longer afford, and it is unconscionable that the Christian churches should continue to make them.

Modernity – drastic and unsettling social change – will always come, whether or not people are ready for the future. Because they will always inflict grievous losses on the vulnerable and unprepared, there will always be a market for apocalyptic visions. However, apocalyptic longings and beliefs are not only the result of various disasters but also their cause. The apocalyptic imagination itself has perpetuated the most vicious and vindictive scenarios of a future in which all the old scores are settled, all differences exorcized from the earth. At the end, one people alone stands in triumph, wounded but heroic, bloodied but vindicated. The apocalyptic imagination dreams of a final solution, and until that dream itself is exposed and repudiated by all who carry it, there will be no way out of the historic cycle of disaster, hatred, and revenge.

Let us consider, first of all, the apocalyptic reaction to modernity. It is a truism that religious extremism is a reaction to social change. Certainly, the modern world does disrupt ways of life that were once relatively reliable, however limited they may have been. Individuals leave familiar contexts where they matter as persons and become role performers. However they may do a job or learn a skill, however they may invest their capital or cast their votes, their uniqueness as persons hardly matters. The machinery of work and politics grinds personal commitments into merely impersonal positions on issues. Loyalty to the state takes the place of a more personal bond between a particular ruler and his or her subjects. The relation of workers to their employers also becomes more self-interested and temporary, because companies are free to abandon workers along with their communities. It does not matter how hard, how long, or how loyally someone has worked, or whether the community has supplied the company with housing, roads, tax relief, and emergency services. Loyalty has become an option that can be cashed in whenever it is convenient to depart. Certainly, the mobility of people and ideas, jobs and money, makes it hard for churches and the nation to hold on to the allegiances of their people.[8] Especially among conservatives there is a fear that the next generation will not sustain the faith or the values of the elders.

Politicians, too, often ignore the value and undermine the viability of their local communities. No wonder that so many conservatives seek to defend these communities from judges appointed by the central government, from school books written by people who do not honor local customs or uphold local moral standards, and from agents of the state who bring deadly force to bear on those who resist the authority of the federal government. The more that people lose their social, emotional, and financial investments, the more tenaciously they cling to their neighborhoods and to the literal meanings of particular words in the Scriptures, in which they are already deeply invested. Some actually form local militias, engaging in survivalist drills and disciplines, and preparing for an Armageddon. As the state itself becomes more intrusive in the lives of local communities, these militant responses grow stronger. And as the state becomes less and less able to maintain a monopoly on legitimate violence in the nation, these militias make an increasingly persuasive claim to popular support.

As social worlds seem to be coming to an end, people turn to apocalyptic literature for telling descriptions of a world that was once familiar and trustworthy but seems filled with corruption, subversion, and the pervasive threat of violence. Secular though many of them are, they are using the language and imagery of the biblical apocalypse to describe what they see as their present and their future.[9]

Modernity seems to dissolve even the local communities that protect individuals from starvation and loss. As Philip Lamy (1997: 104) puts it, the flows of global capital 'will require Americans to share their wealth and resources more equitably with the rest of the world, inevitably resulting in the lowering of the living standards of Americans to those of the Third World.' Powerful international forces inflict irreversible losses on people shorn of the protections of the state. Not long ago the workers in the USA were worried about jobs and capital leaving the country to go south of the border. Now Mexican workers are rightfully afraid that their jobs are fleeing for a new haven of cheap labor and low regulation in China. It is no wonder that Christian extremists in the USA want America to protect its workers.

Would it not be better to point the finger at the Islamic right, and especially to those leaders who promise a day of apocalyptic satisfaction to their long-beleaguered and humiliated followers? Indeed, it was from a world saturated in Christian and Jewish apocalyptic that the early Islamic writers picked up their own beliefs in a final day when all their enemies would be consigned once and for all into Hell. As the Islamic scholar Mahmoud Ayoub puts it, Shi-ite 'eschatology, while remaining within the Islamic framework, resembles the eschatology of post-Biblical Judaism and of the early Christian church.'[10] Regrettably, the wells of the Islamic tradition have been poisoned from the outset with the Jewish and Christian dream of glory. It is therefore all the more necessary for the Christian community to divest itself of all its apocalyptic pretensions to final triumph and vindication at the end of history.

Apocalyptic beliefs interpret current social changes and conflicts in terms of ancient fears and hatreds. The apocalyptic imagination intensifies current grievances by remembering ancient injuries. The apocalyptic vision creates prophecies of future conflict that are potentially catastrophic in their self-fulfilling consequences. For the Christian community to keep apocalyptic beliefs as an article of orthodox faith and as an element of their sacred literature makes the burdens of modernity intolerable. It also confirms Islamic fears that Christians dream of a final solution culminating in the triumph and vindication of Christianity.

Holy enthusiasm for victory and revenge has long sustained the apocalyptic passions of Christians, but similar convictions were widely current in Classical antiquity long before the Church was born. Writing what has been called 'the oldest sentence in Western European philosophy,' Anaximander, in the middle of the sixth century BCE, asserted that 'the source of coming-to-be for existing things is that into which destruction, too, happens, according to necessity; for they pay penalty and retribution to each other for their injustice according to the assessment of Time' (Cancik 2000: 85).[11] Such an apocalyptic conviction intensified from time to time, especially when cities, destroyed in plague and warfare, left survivors longing for a day when fortunes would be reversed. Like Virgil's Aeneas, they believed that 'the Fates/Hold out a settlement and rest for us. Troy's kingdom there shall rise again' (Book I, *ll.* 280–3; Fitzgerald 2000: 11). They shared with Aeneas the apocalyptic vision of 'the secret fated things to come' (Book I, *l.* 384; Fitzgerald 2000: 12). As in Virgil's *Aeneid*, apocalyptic beliefs have long had their own ideological uses in justifying a right to dominate the world as compensation for catastrophic loss.

Outside the city of antiquity, as today on the outskirts of what was once Hiroshima, one could still find the sacred in the vicinity of tombs and shrines. In such places oracles unveiled the past and the future in spontaneous and powerful speech. To them would come individuals and groups of distressed or militant people who had become tired of waiting for the satisfaction of their grievances. Therefore these oracles employed apocalyptic imagery to express the sufferers' hopes and to heighten their expectations of a final battle between an Eastern and Western city, between subjected people and alien conqueror. On that day old scores would be settled, and the poor would be rewarded, while the rich would be sent away empty-handed. Foreshadowing this battle of cosmic importance there would be signs in the heavens indicating that the order of things was about to be shaken to its foundations. The graves would give up their dead. When the untold agony of the past was finally to have been revealed, there would be no way to resist the demand for a final accounting and the redress of long-standing grievances.

Consider the dangers of an apocalyptic vision among those who have suffered the devastation caused by atomic bombs. To the survivors of Hiroshima, apocalyptic imagery speaks of the unspeakable death of that city, especially when normal speech breaks down (Foard 1997: 15–16).

It is time for the West, and indeed for all Christians, to let the God of battle and revenge die. He has failed them over and over again, and the promised day of delivery has turned out repeatedly to be a catastrophe. So long as the churches and the Christian community maintain this antiquated article of faith, they will continue to foster the cycle of collective punishment and revenge.

There is a precedent for such a theological execution. The peoples of Egypt and Mesopotamia, like the Indo-Europeans stretching from the Indus Valley to Scandinavia, knew of gods who could turn defeat into victory in the middle of cosmic battle. They alone, once their favor had been ensured through praise and sacrifice, could keep chaos at bay, and if they failed, they, too, would in the long run die and be forever forgotten.[12] The gods of the apocalypse, who promise a day of final vengeance and victory, have done enough damage without fulfilling their promises. What is needed is a God who shows what it is like to live and die apocalyptically, and so to stand the test of time in the perennial present. I will return to that subject in the last chapter.

However, it is not only the myth of an apocalyptic future that must die, but the institutions that keep it alive. Remember that the enthusiasts for the apocalypse are themselves standing in an ancient Near Eastern tradition that imagined the new creation or era as beginning with the building of a new temple.[13] If a people could perform their rites in the right way at the right moment, they could also imagine themselves as owning and controlling the passage of time. The social order seemed to end when the ritual order was demolished, and it could begin again only when the believers could come together to perform the necessary sacrifices at the sacred center. No wonder, then, that Christians, Muslims, and Jews continually revise the history and archaeology of the Temple Mount in Jerusalem in order to lay new foundations for their current claims and to undergird their aspirations for future domination. For both faiths, the Mount is where the millennium will begin and the Antichrist will put in his appearance; no wonder that the battles preceding it will take on apocalyptic proportions.[14]

However, no people needs a cultic center to believe in its own ability to transcend the passage of time. Some have believed that they themselves were the temple of God, and in their spirits they could carry forward the connection of the present with both the past and the future. Others have known that they could be in touch with the timeless even in places far remote from the sacred center: places where the wind blows over the grass without leaving a trace of its former presence. In such places a people learns to withstand the winds of time and to bear the brunt of mortality and of the moment. Because they have faith, they no longer need the apocalyptic vision, with its promises of recovery and return, triumph and revenge.

Granted that the apocalyptic tradition is an important part of the collective memory of Islamic, Jewish, and Christian peoples, it nonetheless undermines the capacity to imagine a future that is something more than the past repeated indefinitely over time. Monuments, legacies, genealogies, the tales of heroes and the veneration of founders do not require the mystifications of the apocalyptic imagination to retain their place in collective memory. It is long past time when the Christian community should have renounced its vindictive apocalyptic visions. It is time for that community to require itself to live by the faith of the people of the desert and the grasslands, not through institutions that offer sacred violence on behalf of the community along with a spurious form of innocence. Otherwise, so long as the modern world still holds on to its apocalyptic traditions, the future will simply be an updated version of ancient cycles of destruction.

In the last chapter I argued that the apocalyptic vision terrorizes people, provides ideological justification for authoritarian and aggressive regimes, recycles the memory of former disasters, and makes self-fulfilling prophecies about new cataclysms. The apocalyptic imagination provides perennial opposition to whatever is unprecedented or modern and gives the illusion of continuity with the ancient past. I have also argued that these perennial functions of the apocalyptic imagination have become more relevant and potentially dangerous in a global society in which the state not only intrudes more energetically into the private sphere and into the lives of local communities; the state also progressively fails to protect its people from violence and other dangers, whether these originate abroad or at home. Politicians and prophets have long used apocalyptic beliefs to heighten uncertainty, arouse dread, mobilize heroic energies, call people to sacrifice, and to mount an attack on the human psyche. Under the conditions I have already outlined, therefore, we should not be surprised to find that, along with the usual exhortations to prudence, patience, and self-discipline for a long struggle with the enemies of God, politicians and prophets are increasingly likely to use the apocalyptic vision to justify the immediate use of extreme measures in a final battle with the forces of evil.

Apocalyptic visions imagine a society triumphing at last over a mixture of external and internal threats from alien armies, from plague and famine, and from internal deceit, infidelity, and subversion. Apocalyptic beliefs thus raise a society's confidence that it will prevail in a time of trial. Certainly, they promise that the world will be restored to its former state as soon as the righteous have prevailed. However, the same beliefs keep alive a sense of pervasive threat. They make paranoia into a necessary article of a society's faith. Like the generals who wished to keep alive the imagined threat from the Soviet Union so that Congress would provide more funds for the military, the churches have kept alive the notion of a cosmic threat from which only the Christian faith could offer final protection.

Apocalyptic beliefs have long provided ideological cover for the murderous strategies of groups and communities, regimes and entire nations, and they have been used to terrify people into submission. Armed with an ideology of apocalyptic triumph and revenge, the churches have long endorsed programs of ethnic cleansing, supported civil wars, encouraged dissidents hell-bent on murderous revenge, and sought, through torture and execution, to eliminate the last vestiges of free thinking and belief. In addition, the churches' apocalyptic ideology has encouraged Christian nations to imagine themselves entitled to triumph over all who stand in their way. In a world in which the state is becoming less and less able to protect its citizens from violence originating at home or from abroad, and where the state is also a clear and present danger to the local communities and to the privacy of individuals, apocalyptic beliefs may be used to justify official surveillance, state-sponsored violence, and populist forms of retribution.

The churches' apocalyptic beliefs have allowed them to perform and legitimate such violence while insisting that their actions are not done of their own accord but under a divine mandate that confers a certain innocence on those who carry it out. Only some of that violence has been symbolic and ritualized. Recollecting the sacrifice of Christ, many have thrown themselves on the mercies of the church for absolution and forgiveness and have offered themselves to be a living sacrifice in the Eucharist. In its most liturgical forms, this symbolic violence bestows innocence on those who require such self-sacrifice as well as on those who offer it. However, when the churches bless the instruments of war and the soldiers who wage it, and when religious leaders encourage either the state or populist groups to execute the wrath of God, the blanket of innocence stretches to cover a far wider range of actors and their actions. Thus reads one of the lectures of a fourth-century bishop of Jerusalem instructing the faithful on the Eucharist:

> Then, after the spiritual sacrifice, the bloodless service, has been perfected [the consecration of the bread and wine to be the body and blood of Christ] we beseech God over that sacrifice of propitiation, for the common peace of the churches, for the stability of the world, for emperors, for armies and auxiliaries, for those in

sickness, for the oppressed; and praying in general for all who need help, we all offer this sacrifice.[15]

Tim LaHaye's imagination owes much to the Enoch tradition, which supplies the deep mythology that underlies much of the New Testament. 1 Enoch indeed portrays:

> ... all the sins of the whole world as it was sinking into the abyss and being destroyed with great destruction ... the earth being swallowed up into the great abyss, the mountains being suspended upon mountains, the hills sinking down upon the hills, and tall trees being uprooted and thrown and sinking into the abyss.[16]

More is at stake in the Enoch tradition, however, than the satisfactions of a vindictive religious imagination or of middle-class resentment against the wicked or the faithless who despise the sacrifices made by decent people. At the core of that tradition is the longing to stand the test of time. It is to Enoch that the angel Uriel explains all 'the host of heaven ... the luminaries, the months, the festivals, the years, and the days.'[17] To stand in their presence is no longer to be subject to their movements: no longer aware of the perennial difference between mortality and the eternal cycle of the stars and planets, the times and the seasons, the years and the days. But these hosts are really only the external appearances of the being who is the quintessence of time in all its manifestations. The host of heaven is merely the mediator standing between mortals and the One who is before all time.

The apocalyptic beliefs provide a legitimate way of satisfying brutal urges for revenge and vindication. Their images seem legitimate because they are addressed to those whose sufferings entitle them to such a final and victorious day in a divine courtroom. It is the tears of the innocent and victimized believers, not those of their enemies, which will be wiped away. Imagine the American South, which during and after the Civil War demonized the North and longed for a day when their own virtues would at last be recognized and rewarded before a heavenly tribunal. Imagine the North, which during the Civil War regarded Jefferson Davis as Lucifer and the confederate as the forces of Satan. Forget Lincoln, who reminded both the North and the South that the evil in the land was to be found in all the hearts of his countrymen, both North and South.

It is neither new nor surprising that the churches, Protestant and Catholic alike, should harbor such violent beliefs. Violence has been very close to the heart of the sacred in many cultures, including a partially Christianized Western civilization. Perhaps the first sacred rites were performed on hunting expeditions over the carcass of a quarry that had at last been felled. Momentarily appalled at the lifeless form and at an act with totally irreversible consequences, the hunters may have been awed into silence. They may then have offered prayers or performed signs of contrition, seeking forgiveness from their victim or signs of resuscitation: all this before at last exulting in their triumph. Some scholars have found the residues of human sacrifice in the rites of ancient Israel, but for Christians rituals like the Eucharist have enabled worshippers to re-enact a murder while going through the requisite signs of repentance and receiving their forgiveness. From a psychoanalytic perspective, it has long been recognized that fantasies of final victory and revenge lie behind traditions that require of their adherents the utmost in contrition and self-discipline over a lifetime of obedience. It is a contemporary English psychoanalyst, Christopher Bollas, who has used the phrase 'violent innocence' to describe the refusal of individuals to recognize the hurt they are doing others while claiming simply to be telling their troubles. It is an innocence that takes many forms: inadvertence, setting others up to take a fall, denying the emotional content of what one is saying, refusing to credit another's account of their sufferings. It is an innocence that requires the sort of repression of one's own internal emotions that Bollas finds in the fascist character. This is the sort of innocence that characterizes collective scapegoating, in which a congregation or community, or even an entire people, imagine that the root of their troubles lies in the unwanted presence of others who bear the signs and stigmata of significant difference. The apocalyptic imagination thus promises a day when those differences will be removed: a day on which the sufferings of the innocent will be brought to a joyful end, and the sufferings of the wicked will begin in earnest.

The apocalyptic imagination is intended to terrify. In these visions the familiar harbingers of disaster, such as demons and angels, plague and famine, announce the shape of the future. Thus Pat Robertson today claims the Abrahamic legacy for his followers, consigns the secular humanists, new-age religionists, and Islamic opposition to the world that is already passing away, and looks forward to the final battle which will leave the field to the Christians. Thus homosexuals and civil libertarians, abortion-providers and secular humanists, will be held responsible for the coming apocalyptic terrors. Therefore the churches that keep apocalyptic visions in their doctrinal arsenal are responsible for allowing these weapons to be used to terrify a people into submission.

It is quite natural, after all, to see other people as omens of the future. Old people remind us that we, too, will be facing death, sooner or later.

The immigrant reminds us that a time may well be coming when we may be unemployed. The homeless remind us that one of our worst nightmares is that we should someday be without family or friends, or even shelter over our heads, strangers in a world that was once familiar and welcoming. Halbwachs (1992: 51) points out that: 'People of today concern us with the immediate or far away future. We may anticipate much good but also much bad from the future: both the good and the bad are undefined.' Thus to define the good and the bad for the sake of the future, Nazis identified all those who would not be worthy of entering their millennial Reich and stigmatized them as signs of a future to be avoided at all costs. Jews were therefore deprived of their own liberties, asked to wear identifying marks on their clothing, and further segregated into separate living areas. Six million others also went to the camps reserved for those not worthy to enter the Nazi kingdom.

Apocalyptic visions, Christian or fascist, express loathing and inspire terror. Apocalyptic beliefs simply take this basic logic of apprehension and disgust and turn it into orthodoxy. Until the churches repudiate these beliefs, rather than merely interpret them, they will continue to legitimate viciousness.

Unfortunately, since September 11, 2001, apocalyptic visions of the coming battle with the forces of evil have gained political currency and have legitmated the pre-emptive use of nuclear arms. Given the likelihood that a nuclear holocaust would in fact be an unrepeatable and irreversible end of life on this planet, to divest the churches of their apocalyptic beliefs has become not only more difficult but also more necessary. That is because the willingness of so many American preachers to use the apocalyptic vision to legitimate and reinforce national pretensions makes it even more possible for the government to claim the right to use pre-emptive force and, if deemed necessary, nuclear weapons.

Vast numbers of people in America, and not only the fundamentalists, continue to believe not only in eternal life for themselves but in a day when God will purify the world of the vestiges of evil. Like their Muslim counterparts, Christian fundamentalists have been mobilized by clergy with their own dreams of political glory. Tired of seeing the hands of the nation tied by liberals and secular humanists at home, and by coalitions and international organizations abroad, these 'Christian' leaders have urged the nation to recover its sovereignty for the sake of its world-saving mission. While they are waiting for the end, the likes of Robertson and Falwell are eager to teach the world a lesson in what it means to be a sovereign Christian nation. That lesson includes the right to use nuclear weapons in pre-emptive strikes against those who stand in the way.

The apocalyptic story gives us the last chapter to read at the beginning, before we start the book, and it tells us in advance which characters matter and which will disappear by the end. In the meantime, the characters that do not really matter may as well be dead, since they are part of the secular world that is always and forever passing away. Those whose lives are not taken up in this sacred story are hardly worth telling about, and they certainly will not be remembered.

The apocalyptic message tells us that if we live our lives according to the prevailing myth, we, too, will stand the test of time. Those who fail to fit such a transcendent pattern consign themselves to the secular world that is forever passing away, and eventually to Hell. Only those of us who live in accordance with the larger story and who conform to its plan will stand the test of time. All others will be eliminated in cosmic battle, or consigned to eternal punishment in the next life.

Thus the apocalyptic tradition seeks to provide some antidote to the dread of the future by turning the mere sequence of moments and events into a significant past, present, and future. It offers a sacred history: a myth that binds together the moments of life into a continuous narrative with a beginning, a middle, and a conclusion. Those who are included in the authorized version of such a myth may therefore see their own time on earth as part of this larger and inherently sacred story about 'the last judgment, the coming destruction of the wicked, and the triumph of the righteous ones.'[18] Consider populist writers in the USA such as Tim LaHaye, whose novels about the end-times have reputedly sold over 40 million copies and continue to rank among the bestsellers year after year. In these stories, the most favored souls are spared the tribulations of those who must endure the end-times that precede the final Christian millennium. Of course, these are deeply deserved sufferings, and in the near-term they serve the purposes of the Antichrist, who presents himself as the one who can restore order from chaos, as trees and deserts, airstrips and houses, sink below the surface of the earth. However, in the end, the faithful few will have prevailed.

It is one thing to engage in violence that breeds among its victims a passion for revenge. To engage in violence while denying to the victim a chance to claim the right to revenge is what Gil Baillie identifies as the hallmark of 'sacred violence.'[19] It is violence that refuses to accept responsibility for its actions. It is, after all, divine wrath that is unfolding, and the agents of that heavenly fury are not accountable for their actions. Baillie (1995: 155–6) finds examples of this among the Serbs who killed Muslims, but his prototype of violent innocence is Moses, who slaughters his opposition by saying that not he but Yahweh himself is responsible. Similarly, the enlightened Israelites who had given up their formal observances, but who still occasionally engaged in child sacrifice, felt themselves to be innocent, and it was up to Jeremiah to demand that they own up to what in fact they were doing (Baillie 1995: 181).

It is time for the mainstream Protestant churches to announce that they no longer grant any authority to the apocalyptic tradition, with its visions of a final settling of all accounts and the triumph of God's people over their enemies. Until they do, they will continue to encourage others, like Falwell and Robertson, who have the courage of the liberals' convictions without any of the liberals' second thoughts and doubts about their apocalyptic faith. Unless the churches, Protestant and Catholic alike, come together on this, they will continue to make it legitimate to believe in the end as a time when there will be no non-Christians or infidels. Silent complicity with apocalyptic rhetoric soon becomes collusion with plans for religiously inspired genocide.

From time to time, there have been voices in the Protestant churches calling for some fundamental changes in Christian belief. Remember John Robinson's *Honest to God*? Liberal churches have known for a long time that many of their members and even their clergy cannot believe any longer in a universe with Heaven above and Hell below. Others have called for a Christian ethic that is more flexible and sensitive to the needs of particular people in particular places and times: remember contextual ethics? These are only two of the voices that have shocked and annoyed the fundamentalist Christians who, like the masses of Muslims, continue to believe in the resurrection of the dead, the Day of Judgment, the sending of sinners to Hell and the righteous to Heaven, and the final settlement of old scores with the wicked and unbelievers, when their Lord returns to rule the earth (Amanat 2000: 249). It is time for the churches finally to heed these demands for fundamental reforms in theology and in the canon of Scripture itself.

There would be no need for a final Judgment Day if in the meantime societies come to terms with the truth of the past, with all its suffering and injustice. If Americans, for example, decided that now is the time, once and for all, to come to terms with the facts of slavery, and with its legacy of hatred and fear, we would not need to hold out hope for a day of final judgment. If we go to work on plans for redeeming, so far as possible, the losses inflicted on a captive people taken to the USA in chains, we will have nothing to fear on such a day of judgment. It is always time to be accountable for the present, so that the future may begin. The same holds true for all the hidden injuries inflicted on people, not only in America, but wherever American power or neglect has caused suffering. Granted that the steps toward recompense, even when undertaken by the nation itself, will inevitably fail to make other peoples whole. However, such efforts are essential if we are not to continue to live in dread of a day when the nation will be held accountable for the suffering it has inflicted on indigenous peoples, on enslaved captives, and on enemies abroad. However, so long as the nation continues to be comforted by the grandiose apocalyptic visions of the religious right, the USA will continue to reject all limits to its national sovereignty and will continue to impose its will on other nations.

Should we no longer believe in a day when the secrets of the past will be unearthed, as the graves give up their dead, and years of untold agony are finally shouted from the rooftops? Should we abandon hope in a day when those who have deceived others by maintaining the appearance of goodness and righteousness will be exposed for their secret sins and cruelties? Will the truth ever be known? The answer to all these questions is 'Yes,' if every level of government is held accountable for past and present misrule, if corporations are held accountable for past and present fraud and deception and for injurious policies and products, if priests and doctors, lawyers and accountants, are held responsible for withholding and distorting information. Accountability for the past may or may not be beyond the reach of judicial and legal remedies. The point is to bear the burden of time publicly, as a nation. Clearly, by keeping alive hope for a day of revelation at the end of time, the keepers of the apocalyptic dream will continue to defer an accounting in the meantime. Without such an accounting, governments will continue to lie about the costs and the benefits of their policies, corporations will continue to mislead consumers about the safety and effectiveness of their products, and stockholders about their financial condition. Without ongoing accountability, religious and secular professionals will continue to exploit their clients while claiming to serve them. Without such an accounting, the people of the USA will despair that their stories will be heard and honored.

The most overwhelming disasters and defeats threaten to make life totally meaningless unless they are caught up in a larger story. Are the defeated no longer to expect a day of victory? Those who have lost everything in a disaster dream of a perfect time and place where lost loves return and their habitats are finally secure. Are they to abandon their dream? Many exiles have turned calamity and grief into patient anticipation of an ultimate day of victory and return. Does not everyone need a story with a redemptive, even triumphal, end? Otherwise cataclysms could be simultaneously overwhelming and meaningless, and one's end would be of no notice whatsoever. If our lives are not part of a larger story, our deaths will have no meaning. Personal experience will be unrelated to any other moment or event in human experience that might make it significant or memorable. However, that story may be heroic, tragic, and sacrificial without requiring apocalyptic cataclysm in the future through which to avenge and redeem all prior losses. Under the auspices of the religious imagination, a plague in Egypt becomes the beginning of hope that the angel of death will pass by. The murder of an Egyptian task-master by a Jew becomes an event triggering the exodus of the Jewish people from Egypt across the Red Sea and into the wilderness on their way to a better future. The death of a Jewish prophet on a cross becomes the beginning of a new exodus from the slavery that is imposed by the sacred law. To provide such a story of restoration, reversal, and redemption does not require the apocalyptic vision of a final day in which old losses will be redeemed and ancient scores settled. The meek should not delay their inheritance because the churches promise them ultimate vindication at the end of time. With Martin Luther King they may conclude that they have waited long enough. It is chronic delay that produces the longing for Armageddon.

The radical secularization of the apocalyptic imagination will be required if the future is to offer something more than the continuation and repetition of old catastrophes disguised as new battles. Americans have long nourished the memory of their early suffering at the hands of people who unaccountably wished to defend their territory against the incursions of settlers claiming to be the people of God. Such an aggrieved memory nurses the nation's feeling of entitlement to the land and to all its resources, finite though they may be. Until the nation divests itself of its myth of national entitlement, it will continue to feel entitled not only to the lands of the West and the Alaskan north but to oil fields in the Middle East, and it will support Israel's own territorial claims to Gaza and the West Bank, sanctioned as they are by the memory not only of ancient but relatively recent suffering, under the Nazi regime. A radical secularization of collective memory will therefore be necessary if the future is to be different from the past. The first step in that direction is to disable the apocalyptic hope of a day of final vindication and triumph.

To deprive collective memory of the satisfaction of old grievances is going to meet with more than a little resistance. Certainly, apocalyptic visions have preserved the memory of past cataclysms in the form of an impending and disastrous future for nearly three millennia. However, this form of religious vision is like the disease it promises to cure. Apocalyptic prophecies can induce sufficient dread to precipitate a final and disastrous solution to social and personal conflicts. If Western societies wish to stop repeating ancient conflicts, they will have to relieve themselves of the burden of the apocalyptic tradition.

Can this nation free itself from the myth that it shares the history and the destiny of the people of God, that it is a new Israel, and that it is therefore the lead nation? Unfortunately, it is not only the conservative Christian right that sees the USA as the hope of the world. The mainstream Protestant churches have also long married the apocalyptic imagination to the nation's destiny. As James Moorhead put it:

> Having converted technological and material progress into hand-maids of evangelical advance and having conflated the liberty of the Gospel with political liberty and republicanism, they [the Protestant churches] readily identified their nation as the purest exemplar of these trends, and thus styled America, in Ernest Tuveson's phrase, a 'Redeemer Nation ... the contours of history suggested that America had been providentially positioned to fulfill a great millennial destiny.[20]

Thus mainstream Protestants arrived at this peak of national self-satisfaction long before Pat Robertson, who still argues that the world stands or falls with the fortunes and leadership of the USA. It is therefore up to the mainstream Protestant churches to divest themselves of the apocalyptic tradition and its unholy partnership with national chauvinism.

To do this will be difficult in any circumstances, but the more the USA seeks to re-invent itself, the more likely it is to seek guidance and support from an heroic history. As Halbwachs (1992: 86) put it, 'Even at the moment that it is evolving, society returns to its past.' The need to adapt to new situations, to foresee a new future, to realize new possibilities, and to respond to new threats, is sufficiently challenging to throw many a nation back on its own imaginative resources. No wonder that the apocalyptic imagination has flourished in times of uncertainty or change, and that it has renewed currency in the midst of modernity. It is still imperative, however, to find an alternative vision that does not require vindication of claims to extraordinary entitlement, vengeance for past ills, human sacrifice to achieve collective ends, and a final exorcism that removes all sources of difference and opposition. If the mainstream churches can do this, they may once again make a difference to the nation and perhaps also to the world.

Notes

1 'Eschatology: The Doctrine of Last Things' (1978), quoted in *Between Millennia: What Presbyterians Believe About the Coming of Christ*, a publication of the Office of Theology and Worship, The Presbyterian Church (USA), 2001, p. 7.

2 *Between Millennia: What Presbyterians Believe About the Coming of Christ*, a publication of the Office of Theology and Worship, The Presbyterian Church (USA), 2001, p. 4.

3 'Eschatology: The Doctrine of Last Things' (1978), quoted in *Between Millennia: What Presbyterians Believe About the Coming of Christ*, a publication of the Office of Theology and Worship, The Presbyterian Church (USA), 2001, p. 20.

4 *Between Millennia: What Presbyterians Believe About the Coming of Christ*, a publication of the Office of Theology and Worship, The Presbyterian Church (USA), 2001, p. 8.

5 *The Book of Confessions*, 9.11, 9.53–9.56, quoted in *Between Millennia: What Presbyterians Believe About the Coming of Christ*, a publication of the Office of Theology and Worship, The Presbyterian Church (USA), 2001, p. 13.

6 Cf. Ian Paul, 'The Book of Revelation: Image, Symbol, and Metaphor,' in *Studies in the Book of Revelation*, edited by Steven Moyise. Edinburgh and New York: T&T Clark, 2001, pp. 131–148.

7 Cf. David L. Barr, 'Waiting for the End that Never Comes: The Narrative Logic of John's Story,' in *Studies in the Book of Revelation*, edited by Steven Moyise. Edinburgh and New York: T&T Clark, 2001, pp. 101–12.

8 As LeGoff (1992: 43) puts it, 'The revolution in the area of the modern dates from the twentieth century. Modernity, considered up to that point primarily in relation to "superstructures", henceforth takes shape at all levels in the spheres that seem to twentieth-century men (sic) the most important: economics, politics, everyday life, mentalities.'

9 Philip Lamy, 'Secularizing the Millennium, Survivalist, Militias, and the New World Order,' in *Millennium, Messiahs, and Mayhem*: *Contemporary Apocalyptic Movements* edited by Thomas Robbins and Susan J. Palmer. New York and London: Routledge, 1997, pp. 93–119; p. 97.

10 Mahmoud Ayoub, *Redemptive Suffering in Islam*. The Hague, Paris, and New York: Mouton Publishers, 1978, p. 197.

11 G.S. Kirk, J.E. Raven, and M. Schofield (eds), *The Presocratic Philosophers: A Critical History with a Selection of Texts*. Cambridge: Cambridge University Press, 1957, second edition, 1983. Quoted in Hubert Cancik, 'The End of the World, of History, and of the Individual in Greek and Roman Antiquity,' in John J. Collins (ed.) *The Encyclopedia of Apocalypticism*, Vol. 1, *The Origins of Apocalypticism in Judaism and Christianity*. New York and London: Continuum Publishing, 2000, p. 85.

12 Norman Cohn, *Cosmos, Chaos, and the World to Come*: *The Ancient Roots of Apocalyptic Faith*, second edition. New Haven and London: Yale University Press 2001, pp. 50–4.

13 Richard J. Clifford, 'The Roots of Apocalypticism in Near Eastern Myth,' in John J. Collins (ed.), *The Encyclopedia of Apocalypticism*, Vol. I, *The Origins of Apocalypticism in Judaism and Christianity*. New York and London: Continuum Publishing, 2000, p. 12.

14 Gershom Gorenberg, *The End of Days: Fundamentalism and the Struggle for the Temple Mount*. New York, Oxford: Oxford University Press, 2000, p. 17.

15 Cyril of Jerusalem, 'Lecture 5: The Eucharist,' in R.C.D. Jasper and G.J. Cuming (eds), *Prayers of the Eucharist: Early and Reformed*. London: Collins Publishers, 1975, p. 53.

16 I Enoch 83, 4, 7, in Charlesworth (ed.), 1983, pp. 61–2.

17 I Enoch 82, 7, in Charlesworth (ed.), 1983, p. 60.

18 E. Isaac, 'Introduction to 1 (Ethiopic Apocalypse of) Enoch,' in Charlesworth, (ed.), 1983, p. 9.
19 Gil Baillie, *Violence Unveiled: Humanity at the Crossroads*. New York: Crossroad Press, 1995.
20 James Moorhead, 'Apocalypticism in Mainstream Protestantism,' in *The Encyclopedia of Apocalypticism*, Vol. 3, *Apocalypticism in the Modern Period and the Contemporary Age*, edited by Stephen J. Stein. New York: Continuum Publishing, 2000, pp. 72–107; p. 77.

CHAPTER 4

Apocalyptic Visions as Reaction to Disaster

The inability of the modern state to protect its citizens from catastrophe and violence has become more pronounced in a modern world where the flow of ideas and money, of weapons and microbes, is increasingly open to a wide range of users, many of whom are groups with an agenda of violence. At the same time, these groups enable states to project their own powers far beyond their borders, without a serious risk of immediate exposure and retaliation. It is therefore not surprising that apocalyptic beliefs have renewed currency. They reflect the inability of societies to foresee, postpone, and avert disasters, and these beliefs also mirror the exposure of societies to internal sources of subversion. That the three religions in conflict have all developed variations of the same apocalyptic vision makes their enmity all the more inevitable as well as fatal.

The more any society is exposed to internal and external threats, the less it can believe in its own capacity to survive; everyone is suddenly exposed to the passage of time itself. Anything can indeed happen anywhere, and at any time. The world itself seems entirely unreliable: not only dangerous but also deceptive. The appearance of being a safe and thriving land becomes only a façade that hides the threat of death. People live in what Virgil called 'a maze of dread' (*The Aeneid*, Book III, *l.* 67).[1]

Dreams of apocalyptic glory assure a nation that it will triumph over all its enemies, and that in the end all other peoples will either bow in submission and adoration or be eliminated once and for all. However, actual cataclysms destroy these ideological claims to transcendence. Terrible defeats and devastating plagues undermine the conviction that a nation's strengths and virtues will enable it to overcome all dangers and threats; the future becomes an object of dread. The destruction of a city reveals how inadequate were the intelligence services and auguries, prophecies and rites of divination, on which the nation had hitherto depended; the past is not what it used to be. Cataclysms confront an entire people with the possibility that they may become nothing in the end. No wonder they have apocalyptic fantasies of triumphant revenge in the total devastation of their enemies.

Tragically, by holding on to its apocalyptic literature and beliefs, the Christian community keeps such delusions alive. Its apocalyptic visions not only recall ancient cataclysms but expect them to be repeated on a day when ancient scores will be settled once and for all. These self-fulfilling prophecies make it ever more likely that city walls will again be breached, and streets will once more be overrun by foreigners who set fire to the sacred places, loot the treasury, and bring down the houses of the rich and poor alike. Nonetheless, the final battle never comes, because each attempt at retaliation creates the demand for further revenge.

In the midst of a cataclysm, the connection with the past and the future is broken. There is no turning back, because there is nothing left. There is no way to go forward, because prophecy itself has been silenced. In the cities of antiquity, the prophet addressing the crowd was the voice of the people, gathered outside palaces and courts, in stadia and at scenes of execution: the third force alongside the temple and the tribunal. After a city was destroyed, the people therefore turned to the prophetic voice to find words for an experience of devastation that was literally beyond words. No wonder that the prophetic imagination sought to restore some sense of continuity through remembering ancient prophecy and through new prophecies of the apocalypse. Thus the 'Ezra Apocalypse' begins: 'In the thirtieth year after the destruction of our city, I, Salathiel, who am also called Ezra, was in Babylon. I was troubled as I lay in my bed, and my thoughts welled up in my heart, because I saw the desolation of Zion and the wealth of those who lived in Babylon' (IV Ezra, 3, II. 1–2; in Metzger 1983: 528).[2] Deeply troubled in his spirit at the beginning, and able to speak only with great anxiety, toward the end the visionary sees an avenging figure rising from the sea and, with fire streaming from his mouth, annihilating all his enemies, after which Ezra sees himself dictating no fewer than ninety-four books.

As battles destroyed the ancient cities of Asia Minor and the Near East, it was as if the past and the future were imploding into the present. What had long been kept buried was finally revealed: old treacheries and betrayals, undying loves, indeed all the secrets of every heart. Not only did ancient animosities violently erupt in something like a civil war, but alien armies tore down the city walls and invaded every sanctuary. There was no place to hide. Everything that was once held sacred was polluted, even with blood, as the whole society paid for every sin and transgression in its past. Thus Aeneas reflects on the fall of Troy: 'The last day for Dardania has come,/The hour not to be fought off any longer' (*The Aeneid*, Book II, *ll.* 435–6).[3] And in that hour, there is no future other than death itself:

The gods by whom this kingdom stood are gone,/Gone from the shrines and altars. You defend/ a city lost in flames. Come let us die, We'll make a rush into the thick of it./ The conquered have one safety: hope for none ... Grief everywhere,/Everywhere terror, and all shapes of death. (*The Aenead*, Book II, *ll*. 469–73, 490–1)[4]

These are the collective memories of peoples whose memories of disaster have forged a common apocalyptic culture divided, of course, into three major religious traditions. But it is the same dream, the same scenario of utter and final devastation, and the same demand for a final solution that is never quite final.

In the case of Ezra, a calamity had nearly destroyed his spirit and radically undermined his faith in the justice of a God who would allow his chosen people to have been humiliated and destroyed, while the gentiles prospered. That disastrous experience was clearly the destruction of Jerusalem in the civil war of 66–73 CE (Metzger 1983: 520). Like Babylon, Athens, and Alexandria, Jerusalem had been a place where people came to make and to spend money, to pay taxes and offer sacrifices, to find healing and to plead their cases in court, to watch plays, attend contests, and to shout acclaim for their rulers. There the records of old debts were kept, and old scores were to be settled. In cities contests were carried out that symbolized or even literally determined the people's fate. It was to such cities that people brought their hopes and fears, and the destruction of the city therefore meant the loss of much, if not all, that was sacred. The loss of the city would have seemed like the loss of an entire world, and the punishment for such a crime would therefore be imagined as cosmic. Certainly, the destruction of Jerusalem, the good with the evil, the sinners with the righteous, the sanctified with the profane, cast a radical doubt over the justice of God. No wonder Ezra would entertain an apocalyptic vision of Zion and the heavenly Jerusalem, to be established at the end of time.

For centuries now, both Jewish and Christian hope and expectation have been fed by the memory of the Temple and its successive rebuildings. However, the politics of apocalyptic expectation make such memories and hopes inflammable and potentially both self-fulfilling and destructive. They feed the longing for the restoration and rebuilding of the old city, with its way of life, and with its ancient vitality and virtues. So long as the Christian Church continues to sustain ancient hopes and animosities, it will be shaping the future to the past.

Certainly, much of the New Testament makes no sense unless it is read as deriving from an international literature of old grievances and anticipated revenge, in which every battle is part of a larger, cosmic war between East and West, good and evil. The destruction of city-states such as Jerusalem and Athens has fed the Western, as well as the Islamic, religious imagination with apocalyptic images. Apocalyptic literature is full of the names of cities that have been destroyed: Megiddo and Jerusalem, Babylon and Athens. Some of the earliest, Hellenistic oracles remembered and prophesied the destruction of city-states. They looked forward to the day, already past, when 'boastful Greece' would have gone eastward to aid a revolt against Persia, and later Xerxes would have marched westward to invade Greece.[5] Greek cities would attack each other, but then Alexander would renew the ancient contest between West and East, taking Thebes, Tyre, and Babylon, and even earthquakes would continue the devastation (Sibylline Oracles, Book 4, II. 70–89). According to some scholars, this oracle culminates with the vision of a fiery consummation that will leave all cities and rivers 'smoking dust.'[6] As later wars gave the apocalyptic imagination new scores to settle, oracles added Rome, Carthage, Jerusalem, and a wide range of other names to the list of cities slated for final carnage.

Thus visions of a final battle in which historic accounts are to be settled come from moments in history in which entire social worlds were in fact demolished. When city-states like Jerusalem perished in battle, it was a social universe that had been annihilated. In the city of antiquity, courts and temples had continued ancient precedent in law and devotion, had remembered and honored old sacrifices, and had foretold, or at least imagined, the future. They had given a place to the passage of time. Once destroyed, they left the past as well as the future in ruins.

The rites of the court and the temple also prevented mayhem and bloodshed from occurring in the streets, by restricting sacrifice to the times and places ordained for the purpose of purifying the city of its internal dangers. Garrisons guarded the gates of the city and kept watch for threats emerging on the horizon. The fires lit in Jerusalem announcing that the Sabbath had begun were rekindled on hills for miles in all directions, so that a dispersed people could share in the sacred moment originating in the city of God. Time thus began and would eventually end in the sacred city at the center of the universe.

Such a city is pivotal to a society's sense of time. Its rituals 'key' the present to the past and bring the past into the present in order to create and sustain a usable future.[7] When that city is destroyed, however, there is no way to honor the past or foreshadow or forestall the future. There remains only an endless and troubled present, in which it is too late to satisfy old longings or to hope for a future that will be in any way different from the past. All the institutions have perished that could have forestalled a day of reckoning, and recollection constantly feeds the fires of longing for revenge. Without the prospect of reprieve, and in the absence of any form of mediation, anything can happen anywhere at any time. The apocalyptic present is like Jerusalem or Jenin, where there is no alternative to terror and despair. Dante called it hell.

Thus the apocalyptic literature links the times, the present, with a catastrophic past and a cataclysmic future. The present moment is therefore perennially critical. It is always time to make crucial decisions, to purify the society, to rectify wrongs, and to realign the soul with the forces of good rather than evil. The apocalyptic vision excruciatingly intensifies the meaning and experience of time.

Societies develop their own notions about the difference between the human and the bestial, the natural and the unnatural, the noble and the ignoble, but cataclysms destroy public confidence in such distinctions. In the midst of disasters, virgins give birth, and the tombs give up their dead. Darkness comes at noon, and morning prayers are to be said in the evening and evening prayers at dawn (cf. Panourgia 1995: 161). Because the first are then last, and the last first, it is no longer clear who or what should take precedence. Traditional priorities seem strangely irrelevant, even meaningless. As a city is being destroyed, no one cares about seniority, rank, and authority. At the most, there is a milling crowd, in which even a little child can be the leader, and a single voice may galvanize the entire throng into precipitous action. The community becomes a lynch mob in which unthinkable things are done, and there are no witnesses, no records, no testimony by which to assign responsibility for horror and death. There is no time or occasion for the conventional funeral procession: no time to incorporate the memory of the dead into the community of the living.

Consider, for example, the pillage and rape, arson, and murder of the urban Tamil and Indian population during the riots in Sri Lanka in 1983. There the soldiers and police, along with the urban unemployed, acted as one. It was difficult even to tell the monks from the laity (Tambiah 1992: 75). Cataclysms are thus commemorated in apocalyptic visions of a millennial society in which there is no distinction between genders and classes; all share the common fate. At the time of the Sri Lankan riots, the Buddhist monks, especially the radicalized ones, developed a millenarian ideology, in which the virtues of a peasant, agrarian past were to be restored in a new society. Thus old social distinctions between the rich and the poor would once and for all be destroyed, and social life would be open and fluid (Tambiah 1992: 91).

Moreover, in the midst of a cataclysm, no place, no objects or symbols, remain to link the living with the dead: no shrines, heirlooms, homesteads, emblems. All connection with the past is severed. Because the past no longer offers any precedent for the living, the survivors are in an entirely new situation that seems wholly unique and unprecedented. As for the future, it is opaque but has already begun. With no end in sight, people despair, lose their will to live, and their souls begin to perish within them. To give meaning to such a cataclysm is absolutely necessary if people are to feel that they have not lost everything that could give them a sense of continuity with the past.

After a cataclysm, however, the present becomes less of an anomaly without a relevant past or an imaginable future. Survivors therefore search the past for a precedent: a plague or invasion, a flood or drought that decimated the community in an earlier generation or epoch. The apocalyptic vision assures people that they are no longer living in an unprecedented time, but are instead linked with the experiences of ancestors and heading toward consummate satisfaction in the future.

At the very least, apocalyptic ambitions are simply an agonized response to human sorrow: a sign of hunger for restoration. When Ezra encounters a woman in grief for her only son, whose sudden death has driven her to seek death through sorrow and fasting, he compares her grief unfavorably with his own and with that of the people of Israel:

> For Zion, the mother of us all, is in deep grief and great humiliation ... our sanctuary has been laid waste, our altar thrown down, our temple destroyed, our harp has been laid low, our song has been silenced, and our rejoicing has been ended; the light of our lampstand has been put out, the ark of our covenant has been plundered, our holy things have been polluted, and the name by which we are called has been profaned; our free men have suffered abuse, our priests have been burned to death, our Levites have gone into captivity, our virgins have been defiled, and our wives have been ravished; our righteous men have been carried off, our little ones have been cast out, our young men have been enslaved and our strong men made powerless. And what is more than all, the seal of Zion – for she has now lost the seal of her glory, and has been given over into the hands of those who hate us. (IV Ezra 10:II. 7, 21–25; in Metzger 1983: 546–7)

Finally, the grieving woman, who had lost her son, is transformed into a vision of the New Jerusalem, and Ezra's sorrow is now relieved by the perennial dream of restoration and return. Like Ezra, in the aftermath of a cataclysm, survivors rummage through the past for prophecies, precedents, and prologues: for anything that would suggest that they are not living in a time wholly beyond the human imagination.

The limited catastrophe of September 11, 2001 created a renewed demand for rites that can link the present with the past and the future and that bind the living to the dead in bonds of sacred memory. On the day of the bombing itself, New Yorkers crowded the churches for one service after another, and there they heard in psalm and story the rhetoric of death and resurrection, of a city destroyed and yet to be reborn, of purifying fires and rededicated souls, and of a God whose wrath is the prelude to His mercy.

However, it is not enough to understand the sorrow that gives rise to the apocalyptic imagination. Apocalyptic beliefs in a day of vicious retribution justify hopes not merely for recovery and restitution but also for retribution and revenge. Christian, Jewish, and Islamic apocalypticism therefore continues to project ancient conflicts between peoples and civilizations into a future day of judgment, when these conflicts will dissolve in a final exorcism of all social and cultural difference. So long as sins must be paid for, and grievances must be satisfied, there will be no way to break the cycle of transgression, retribution, and revenge. So long as Christians, Jews, and Muslims continue to entertain apocalyptic beliefs, they will be responsible for the tragic results of these self-fulfilling prophecies.

Because they are made legitimate by religious authority, apocalyptic beliefs give many societies reason to become paranoid. Sometimes danger will seem to come from alien cities and empires, from infidels and their more fanatic followers. Sometimes danger will seem to come from within, from people who look familiar, but who are in fact agents for an enemy system. The arch-typical enemy in apocalyptic visions is therefore someone like the Devil or the Antichrist, who wears disguises to make him seem familiar, safe, and benign, but who poses the ultimate danger to all who come under his spell. The usual apocalyptic suspects are therefore not only ghosts and other super-human aliens, but suspicious strangers of all kinds who have become domesticated. When it is difficult to separate the native from the foreign, the good from the bad, surveillance will increase, along with preparations for war. According to the apocalyptic vision, it is only when the final battle is fought that the true face of the enemy will be revealed.

So it was in the massacres of Tamils in Sri Lanka in 1983, when tens of thousands were killed who had made a vital contribution to Sri Lankan society. The purpose of the speeches and ceremonies that followed, Spencer (1990: 238) tells us, was 'to demonstrate underlying continuity, eternal verities, in the face of change and disruption.' In the aftermath of the Sri Lankan riots, as Spencer (1990: 239) goes on to argue, people similarly tried to transform a terrifying and chaotic moment into an event with meaning, and to deny that a radical break in the passage of time had occurred. It is this very denial that is at the heart of the apocalyptic vision, that links the past to a future of inevitable but legitimate destruction.

Apocalyptic visions thus make cataclysms seem to have been predetermined by some fatal cause or chain of events. Perhaps the sins of previous generations or an earlier act of apostasy delivered the city to the wrath of the gods. Perhaps an earlier transgression of the boundaries between the sacred and the profane, between the human and the super- or sub-human, or between the generations and genders, caused the present, horrific loss of all boundaries separating order from chaos. After the fall of Jerusalem in the sixth century BCE, prophets argued that the sins of the people had caused their exile. Again, after the destruction of Jerusalem in the first century CE, some voices attributed the city's fate to the aggression of the people of Israel against their neighbors. When Jerry Falwell attributes the bombing of Washington and New York City to secularists, feminists, and homosexuals, he was merely echoing these retroactive prophecies that add guilt and shame to the burden of grief. So long as the Christian churches continue to honor apocalyptic literature as part of Scripture, they will continue to color cataclysms in the hues of the legitimate and the inevitable.

I have been arguing that at first cataclysms destroy the connection between the present, the past, and the future. The past is gone forever; the future imminent but indecipherable. Because the present is therefore overwhelming and meaningless, pundits and prophets search the past for precedent, prophecy, and explanation. In retrospect, what had been hidden for years seems finally to have come to the surface in the destruction of the city. Ancient transgression has been punished. Old grievances have been satisfied. Scores have been settled, and bills paid. The violence underlying the foundations of the city has been unearthed, and the ancient crimes, perhaps of fratricide or patricide, have emerged at last. Thus the past has caught up with the present. As for the future, it, too, has begun with a vengeance, before anyone could prepare for it, and it will end in revenge.

To enable people to prevent another implosion of the past and the future into the present, the Church offers its services of ritual. These rites provide little, carefully staged apocalypses. In the Eucharist, for instance, an apocalyptic moment is staged again and again, such as the death of Christ on the cross. In that overwhelming moment the past and the future imploded into the present, and there was darkness at noon. The orders of precedence on earth were reversed, the first were last, and time itself literally would never be the same again. In the Greek Orthodox liturgy, the priests remain hidden behind a screen, where the awful sacrifice is performed outside the view of the people, and it is only when the priests emerge in front of the screen, or *templum*, that the full force of the moment is revealed in the symbolic remains of the one whose death changed everything (cf. Panourgia 1995: 102). The irreversible passage of time is reversed, and the end becomes a beginning.

Ritual offers a pseudo-mastery over the passage of time. Various rites introduce symbolic enactments of death and the disruption of time in tolerable amounts that require anticipatory or retrospective grieving. The church year revolves around preparations for the death of Christ and in recollections of his final suffering. In these programmed words and deeds, rituals bring the past and the future together in a single moment without dissolving the community into chaos. The past becomes coeval with the present, and the dead come back, although not yet with a vengeance. Old grievances are satisfied symbolically, rather than in the wholesale bloodshed of a cataclysm. Even the future is allowed a partial and temporary appearance, as in the case of the Christian Eucharist, which is an eschatological meal. In all these ways a ritual dramatizes a social order that is proof against the passage of time, as the church administers apocalyptic terror in small but medicinal doses.

One antidote to the abrupt and devastating intrusion of the final days is thus to take part in times and occasions that offer therapeutic amounts of the unique and irreversible: days of solemn obligation, of sacrifice and repentance, of the memory of rescue and of petition for saving graces. In the Christian churches much of the sacred calendar is thus taken up with seasons of anticipation for dreadful events: preparations for the coming of a Savior whose advent reverses the usual orders of precedence, levels the mountains, exalts the valleys, exposes the secrets of the heart, and releases the dead from their graves.

Sacred calendars and the schedule for religious observance seek to provide an antitoxin against destruction. On days of repentance and commemoration, particularly disastrous events are remembered and prayers are offered for deliverance from the final cataclysm. Thus the people may venerate one who returned from the dead, or they may welcome, if only on the proper occasions, the souls of the departed who are allowed periodic but brief returns to the company of the living. In these rites, time still erodes the hope of permanence. The dead are known to be present in ways that also signify that they are ephemeral: of the day, of the moment, *epi-hemera*, and therefore subject to the very immediate passage of time. Thus rituals provide brief encounters with the uniqueness of the moment and the irreversibility of time itself even while telling a story of continuous progress toward a future redemption of the past.

In an attempt to make horrendous death imaginable and to give it precedent, rituals thus lay the groundwork for interpreting or even explaining cataclysmic events by placing them back into the sequence of what came before and will come after. However, as alternatives to apocalyptic terror, rituals offer no immunity to cataclysm but only the flimsy protections of sympathetic magic. These ritualized attempts to turn the tables on the passage of time, notably, fail to work when the scale of death is overwhelming, as in times of plague or famine, of war or natural disaster. In such cataclysms the full force of time is literally overwhelming. Every attempt at prognostication and prediction, at interpretation and explanation, therefore fails to give the event a believable place in the society's lexicon for disaster. In such a cataclysm, death is so overwhelming, and the moment so disruptive, that the past is irrelevant, useless, or even forgotten, and the future seems inconceivable, impossible. That is why an English parish church in Surrey, self-styled as the Church of the Apocalypse, like other churches has a clock on its tower, but in this church the face of the clock is entirely covered.

When rituals fail to provide medicinal amounts of preventive terror, the apocalyptic imagination takes over. It is thus no accident that in the United States the apocalyptic imagination informs public entertainments and popular books, when at the same time the churches are having difficulty distinguishing good from bad priests, conservationists argue over the difference between native and foreign species, the courts and the government disagree over the status of immigrants and alleged terrorists, and movies demonstrate that it is sometimes hard to distinguish the true aliens from the local citizens. Especially when sacrifices fail to avert danger and death, or when rituals fail to create faith and obedience among the young or to domesticate women, the apocalyptic imagination reveals that all of these dangers, internal and external, may threaten the very survival of the society.

During times of collective disaster, rituals conspicuously fail to help individuals to bear the stigma of time. The world is then full of souls whose lives have been blighted or who have suffered deaths that were premature, sudden, and ugly, and who have no place in the safe havens of collective memory offered by the church. Nancy Caciola (2000: 66, in Gordon and Marshall 2000) writes of 'the displaced dead who wandered, restlessly, through the imaginations of late medieval urban communities. Their memories ... their ghosts ... lingered on amidst the community of the living; searching out, and sometimes finding, a physical place in which to lodge.' Plagues and the destruction of entire communities or even cities place the living and the dead together in the same spiritual community.

Can conversation fill the void of meaning without the mediation of clergy and the formal framework of a rite? In her discussion of folk responses to the death of a member of the family, for instance, Neni

Panourgia (1995: 78–9) describes a conversation in which various relatives and acquaintances sought to explain the death of her uncle: the explanations ranging from witchcraft and Satanism to the providence of God or the workings of depression. Death, even such an ordinary and expected death, was still an interruption of the other world into this one and required the mediation of commentary. The advent of what Panourgia calls 'the ultimate unsame, the final nonself' plunged the living into conversations intended to restore the connection of the present with both the future and the past. Our last, best hope may be in talking with each other and with our enemies, in the midst of grief.

When apocalyptic fervor cannot be adequately domesticated in the church or satisfied in public ceremony but instead feeds collective enthusiasms, apocalyptic prophecies become self-fulfilling. No longer able to place the memory and dread of cataclysmic events in a longer time-span, apocalyptic prophecy announces and hastens the advent of a day when destruction and the settling of accounts is always imminent.

Only when it is adequately ritualized can apocalyptic imagery relegate wholesale slaughter and destruction to the distant past or forestall it in the meantime by sacrifice and obedience. Indeed, the purpose of rites and sacrifices is not only to remember past cataclysms but to ensure that the angel of death will indeed pass overhead and destroy the first born of some other people. So long as the proper dues are paid and rites performed, and so long as the city and the people stay in their assigned courses, the dreaded day of cosmic battle will be forestalled.

It is therefore not surprising that in the weeks immediately after the bombing of the World Trade Center, many Americans returned in greater numbers to the synagogues and churches, to concert auditoriums and sports arenas: public occasions for commemorating the dead, singing familiar hymns and anthems, and renewing commitment to the future. Ritual is indeed the last line of defense against the passage of time: the final repudiation of the unprecedented and irreversible character of moments and events.

After September 11, many commentators fulfilled the traditional function of the scribal community by searching the past for precedent and prediction: for the meaning of signals and messages, of clues and signs, that many had noticed but which relatively few had explicitly understood or announced. Some explored the likelihood of there being another such disaster or perhaps even a worse one in the foreseeable future, while others discussed the ways in which to rebuild the towers and to commemorate the deaths that still haunt the site. Indeed, the attempt continues to lessen the sense that what happened on September 11 was not only unique and unprecedented but also unrepeatable and irreversible. By reviewing the past, and by projecting not only disaster but the possibilities of reconstruction and revenge into the future, such efforts at commemoration and anticipation seek to create or renew a narrative that overcomes the break with the past, softens the impact of the moment with the balm of precedent and recollection, and makes the future seem less opaque and frightening.

Of course, today the public relies less on liturgy and the clergy than on the networks, the news channels, the television commentators, and the politicians to continue to enshrine the memory of disasters like the bombing of the World Trade Center and to prophesy about future disasters. However, the mass media offer no rites of prevention and intensify the public's dread of danger from a wide range of sources, from microbes to terrorists. Constant replays of the bombings of the World Trade Center and Pentagon can also intensify public demand for revenge and create a mass market for apocalyptic visions of a day of final triumph. Thus the media may indirectly increase the likelihood of further cataclysms.

Some will argue that the apocalyptic imagination alone seems adequately realistic in times of terrible cataclysm: the fall of the Roman Empire and the invasions of the Vandals; during periods of earthquake, plague, and flood; again after the failure of the Carolingian Empire to reincarnate Rome; as the Normans were invading England, and while the Turks were expanding their domains in Armenia and the eastern Mediterranean; during the sixth-century mission from the Roman Church to England and in the Crusades of the eleventh and twelfth centuries from England to Jerusalem; during the Reformation and the revolutions of the sixteenth and seventeenth centuries, when there were millennial movements in England and on the Continent, with both Christians and Jews claiming to be the messiah; during the settlement of New England, as there had been somewhat earlier during the Spanish conquest of the peoples of Central and Latin America.[8] During such periods there is a mass market for reassurances that there will be no more danger of running out of time, because neither subversion from within nor pollution from outside, neither disaffection nor disloyalty, infidelity or betrayal, will ever again undermine the walls of the city. No enemy from the outside will ever again be able to storm the gates or defeat the armies of the faithful. The city will prevail, forever. There will no longer be any danger from the unique or the novel, since the city that is revealed on the final day will turn out to have been ordained from the very beginning; neither will there be any more future, since the last day has finally come.

Like the use of sympathetic magic to fight fire with fire, the apocalyptic imagination fights time with time itself: with time that has been raised to the highest of all possible powers. The apocalypse therefore would appear to be a cure that is really tantamount to the disease for which it is the alleged remedy. However, apocalyptic visions are less the cure than the disease because these visions evoke a disastrous day whose coming will be sudden, final, and irreversible: the end of time. Prophets thus speak of a day that comes like a thief in the night, or with the blast of a trumpet, suddenly and with fateful consequences for all except the superbly well prepared. Such visions of the end evoke the surprise of the unprecedented, the bewilderment that accompanies the discovery of the unique, the sense of despair that comes when one knows that it is too late to recover or to undo the past.

Others may argue that apocalyptic imagery is not terrifying to the vast majority of Americans. That is because mainstream Protestants have lost view of the end and feel immune to its sudden appearances. However, millions of others have not been so fortunate. Many daily encounter terror and death, and for them apocalyptic religion has long provided the necessary framework for understanding the connection between their present, their past, and their future. For those described by Orlando Patterns in *Rituals of Blood*, the future has come anywhere at any time in the form of a burning cross or hangman's rope, as Christians entertained themselves with scenes from the Last Judgment. For many, the modern continues to be the sphere of the sudden and untoward, the new and the disruptive: the time in which everything solid has melted, if not by the forces of capitalist production, then by mob action. For those with little confidence in their ability to control the future, the apocalypse still offers the prospect of revelation and revenge.

No wonder that the apocalyptic imagination appeals to those whose grievances over past injustice have not been assuaged. For them an apocalyptic future offers the only guarantee that their present and past sacrifices will someday be redeemed. As Maurice Halbwachs once asserted, 'We can evoke places and times that are different from those in which we find ourselves because we place both within a framework which encompasses them all.'[9] For many, that framework has been the apocalyptic vision, and in a nuclear age many more may grasp it with renewed interest and enthusiasm. That is precisely my point. In a nuclear age, the apocalyptic delusion can bring disaster in equal measure to those who hold it as to those against whom it is directed. Even for the poor, nuclear warfare would finally deprive them of any chance for a final triumph and vindication. It is therefore crucial that collective memory relegate apocalyptic religion to the literature of a discredited fiction. Otherwise demands for final recompense will continue to be shaped by self-fulfilling prophecies of collective suicide.

Notes

1   Fitzgerald, 2000: 67. As Aeneas and his retinue leave their land, they face the future with the scant protection of prior visions: 'Our minds were turned by auguries of heaven/To exile in far quarters of the world;' however, the screen on which the future was projected offered little detail or reassurance: 'none could say where fate/ Would take or settle us ... [and they] hoist sails to the winds of destiny' (Book III, *ll.* 5–6, 8–9, 13).[46] No sooner, however, than the future seemed about to begin than they encountered a terrifying reminder of the past, still present and unfulfilled, in a place where they would have least expected to encounter it. As Aeneas tries to construct an altar on which to offer a sacrifice for divine protection, he gathers what appear to be saplings, but their appearance of young vitality conceals a body, long dead but still containing the spirit of a Trojan emissary slain there by those to whom he had been sent for help in relieving the siege of Troy. Thus the past comes back to haunt the living precisely when it can no longer be revisited or retrieved and throws into doubt a future that is as opaque as it is immediate and pressing on the present. That is why Aeneas found himself 'in a maze of dread.'
2   'The Fourth Book of Ezra,' translated, edited, and with an introduction by B.M. Metzger, in James H. Charlesworth, *The Old Testament Pseudepigrapha*, Vol. I, Garden City, New York: Doubleday, 1983, pp. 517–559, p. 528.
3   Fitzgerald, 1990, p. 45.
4   Fitzgerald, 1990, p. 46.
5   These after-the-fact prophecies are typical of some of the oracles from which the early apocalyptic literature was derived, and we are to understand that they were intended to add credibility to the prophecies that the apocalyptic narrator then made about the future, often in the service of some dynastic ambition. Cf. Richard J. Clifford, 'The Roots of Apocalypticism in Near Eastern Myth,' pp. 12–15.
6   J.J. Collins, Introduction to Book 4, in Charlesworth (ed.), 1983, p. 381.
7   Barry Schwartz, 'Memory as a Cultural System: Abraham Lincoln in World War II,' *American Sociological Review*, Vol. 61, Issue 5 (Oct. 1996): 908–927; see p. 911.
8   Eugen Weber, *Apocalypses: Prophecies, Cults, and Millennial Beliefs Through the Ages*. Cambridge, Mass.: Harvard University Press, 1999, pp. 34, 48ff.
9   Maurice Halbwachs, *On Collective Memory*, edited, translated, and with an introduction by Lewis A. Coser. Chicago and London: University of Chicago Press, 1992, p. 50.

CHAPTER 5

The Apocalyptic Attack on the Self

It is too late to hope that merely reinterpreting apocalyptic beliefs will make them less dangerous to the human community. Origen regarded the apocalypse of John, for instance, as an allegory, and Bishop Augustine of Hippo made it clear that he thought the process of apocalyptic purification should take place slowly over time through a variety of penitential and devotional disciplines (Weber 1999: 44–5). Thus over a thousand years later John Donne writes, 'What if this were the world's last night?/ Mark in my heart, O soul, Where thou dost dwell,/The picture of Christ crucified, and tell/ Whether that countenance can thee affright, ...'[1] It is the same apocalyptic vision that inspired American Protestants in the nineteenth century to believe that their own struggles with sin were part of the larger historical, even cosmic drama of salvation. As James Moorhead points out, '... the struggle surrounding each believer's conversion was for the believer a premonition of the final battle between Christ and Antichrist.'[2]

Even the more pragmatic and secularized visions have easily become a program for imposing the community's will on the individual's psyche. Some religious traditions indeed predicate apocalyptic hope on a lifetime of self-abnegation and require the renunciation of all individual markers of uniqueness, significance, and distinction. In return, the apocalyptic imagination offers a wide range of narcissistic satisfactions, from vindication to triumph and revenge, but these will finally come only to those who are willing to surrender to the divinity all grounds for invidious distinction, and all traces of a unique and unprecedented self. Apocalyptic triumphs are promised to those who temporarily renounce their sense of superiority and their desire for a final exaltation that lifts them above the mass of humanity. One might think that such a discipline would make apocalyptic visions less destructive in the long run. However, the faithful will still prevail on the last day, and then they may enjoy the prospect of witnessing all others disappear or suffer the agonies of the faithless and the damned.

Under the auspices of the Church, the apocalyptic tradition has therefore spawned a variety of disciplines of the soul that require penance, renunciation, asceticism, and self-mortification over a lifetime in order to prepare the soul for the final judgment. What Max Weber thought was the Protestant ethic, a rigorous lifestyle of self-discipline and long-term planning, was in fact a transformation of the apocalyptic vision into a long period of temptation, testing, and trial. This ascetic discipline, this-worldly and pragmatic, derives from a more mystical form of self-immolation in the hope of liberating the soul from its captivity to an alien power. John Donne tells God that his soul is 'betrothed unto your enemy,' and he begs God to repossess his soul and to free his reason of its captivity as well. The image of being possessed is further spelled out as Donne compares his soul to a place that has fallen into alien hands. Donne begs God to take him back by force: 'I, like an usurped town, to another due,/ Labour to admit you, but oh, to no end,/ ... Take me to you, imprison me, for I/Except you enthrall me, never shall be free,/ Nor ever chaste, except you ravish me.'[3] Note how the image of a city fallen into enemy hands becomes a way of speaking of the soul's captivity and its need for redemption. In order to save the city of the soul, it is necessary to destroy it.

A longing for a spiritual exorcism calls for a siege of the psyche itself. As Donne's image of the captive city illustrates, the apocalyptic vision came out of the disasters in which ancient city-states were destroyed, their people sold into slavery or sent into exile, and their gods discredited. It is this memory, as I have argued in the previous chapter, that underlies the earliest apocalyptic literature, with its long lists of cities that have been destroyed and that in the future will be punished with far worse devastation. Now I am arguing that *the same apocalyptic vision has been used to mount an assault on the psyche*. The enemy must be driven from the deep interior of the psyche to rid the self of whatever makes it singular and alone rather than an image of its original.

The apocalyptic vision sees the self as being held captive, as seeking immolation, and as longing for transformation and release from captivity to other spirits. The apocalyptic vision also promises release from the guilt of unmet obligation, and from the sense of having failed the aspirations implanted by high ideals. When individuals long for the revelation of their own truth and worth, they may tire of living in the meantime: the time when all judgments are suspended and the worth of the individual remains unknown. Thus Donne defends the right of the Christian to seek a holy death of his or her own volition rather than to wait for death to be imposed on the individual by nature or by a magistrate. Nothing is more important than the preparation of the soul for reunion with God. To that end the Christian 'withdraws and purges his body from all corruptions and delivers it from all pollutions, venom, and malign machinations of his (and God's) adversaries and prepares it by God's inspiration and concurrence for the glory that, without death, cannot be attained!'[4] This final battle with the enemies of God is a cosmic battle, and the individual's soul stands to lose, with all the enemies of God, unless it remains firmly committed to the radical exorcism of all pollutions that stand between the soul and the purity of God alone. The Christian thus turns the apocalyptic imagination into a way of self-mortification and of death. In the new Jerusalem, the individual will show that he or she has stood the test of time.

For entire societies, as for individuals, mortality and cataclysm become necessary conditions for final vindication and triumph. In the end the gods will have been restored to their proper place, the honor of the line vindicated, the crisis overcome. The society will have withstood the passage of time, and its heroes will have been immortalized in popular piety and official recollection. To achieve such an end, of course, requires souls dedicated to the vision, wills inured to self-sacrifice, and ready if necessary to die for the nation.

Earlier I noted that Pat Buchanan fears that without new infusions of youthful blood, America is going to die. Buchanan therefore wants to instill more patriotism in American youth so that they will become dedicated to the nation and ready for self-sacrifice. To live, therefore, the nation must undergo a major spiritual and moral rebirth. Thus Buchanan wants American history to be reborn in the public and private schools of America. There the civil war must be retold in a way that will honor the sacrifices of both sides. He wants American history to be taught so that the young will recall the expansion into the West for its heroism and creativity rather than only for the displacement and destruction of indigenous peoples. Rhetorically, Buchanan (2002: 152) asks, 'Were wrongs committed and crimes covered up? Surely. That is true of every nation. ... [But] With a growing love of country comes a growing desire to be forever a part of this people, and a willingness to sacrifice, even to die, to defend this people, as one would defend one's family.' Thus Buchanan prophesies the death of America in order to instill renewed demands for self-sacrifice.

The same motif of social decay appears in Hal Lindsey's apocalyptic epic, *The Late Great Planet Earth*, in which he asks rhetorically whether there has 'ever been a time when the potential for self-destruction was as great as it is today' (Lindsey 1970: 101). Obviously he is referring to collective self-destruction, for which the remedy is a mortal struggle with one's own soul. Time is running out on America because of an array of ills, only some of which have to do with the facts of overpopulation and the degradation of the environment.[5] In Lindsey's view, not only is crime going up, but the country faces a wide range of threats, from guerrilla warfare to illiteracy. Further, the spread of cities and the vast complexity of a computerized society call for ever more surveillance and control.

In the previous chapter I noted how defeats and cataclysms made people long for a day when they would be able to redeem their old losses and triumph over ancient enemies. Apocalyptic visions imagine such a day, but that day also offers a terrifying prospect of trials and carnage. In the feast of the Passover the priesthood not only institutionalized the memory of ancient cataclysm, the plague that destroyed the first born of the Egyptians but not of the Jews; it also foreshadowed the day of eventual destruction from which at least the faithful would be saved if, and only if, they made the necessary sacrifices.

Rituals thus prepare the individual for sacrificial commitment.[6] Like the Lincoln Day ceremonies performed during the worst days of the Second World War, such ritual inspires sacrifice and offers hope of transcendence and victory in the long run.[7] By promising divine rescue in return for self-surrender, rituals instill a willingness to sacrifice the self for the good of the larger society and its destiny. The churches are in no position to regard Lindsey and the Christian right with contempt, having themselves long used the prospect of apocalyptic torments to terrify souls into submission. Take, for example, this description of what a devout layperson would have found in a late medieval English church:

> Any parishioner sitting or standing in the nave and looking towards the high altar in the chancel could be left in no doubt as to the core of the faith and the fate of his or her soul when time should end, as it would. The rood, surmounting the screen separating nave from chancel, comprised a carved figure of Christ crucified, flanked by the Virgin Mary and St. John, an echo in visual form of the truth celebrated in the mass – celebrated with most circumstance at the high altar in the chancel beyond. This representation of the Passion had broader ramifications of reinforced meaning for it would, in all probability, have been set in a fuller visual context intended to remind the onlooker of the Judgement when the individual's response to Christ's sacrifice would be decided: roods were frequently set within a Doom painted on the surrounding chancel arch, with St. Michael weighing souls under God's gaze, whilst the saved on one side ascended to the celestial city and the damned on the other were tossed or dragged into Hell's mouth. (Burgess 2000: 46, in Gordon and Marshall 2000)

When the savior returns as a judge, one's protector becomes a potential destroyer. The intention is to school the soul in self-mortification.

The churches have thus encouraged self-mortification as a way of avoiding the terrible torments of the Last Judgment. Of course, souls must die to their natural selves in order to enjoy during their lifetimes a foretaste of life eternal, and they must share in the sufferings of Christ, re-enacted in the liturgy at the high altar, if they are to be spared the worst on the Last Day. However, with enough confession and repentance, individuals can prepare their souls for the trials of the Last Day.

Medicinal doses of apocalyptic terror thus provide the tonic necessary to stimulate self-mortification. That is why apocalyptic visions hold out the prospect of a 'second death' worse than the first: the death that comes from being plunged forever into the fires of hell (Bernstein 1993: 255). To avoid that fate one can then live an entire life of self-purification and self-mortification, as if one could destroy hell by imitating it. The Church has never been slow to exploit this remedy against despair as a great incentive to discipline (Bernstein 1993: 251).

The churches may argue that they, after all, have long ago revised the notions of the apocalyptic in favor of the idea that the millennium had already been initiated in the time of Christ or of the early Church. All it required was a continuing reformation of the heart and the soul. However, as Reiner Smolinski (2000: 39) points out, the English theologian Joseph Mede, following Johann Heinrich Alsted of Germany, broke with the revisionist notion. Instead, they argued, the apocalypse was yet to come and would be inaugurated by the 'literal and corporeal resurrection of Christ's martyrs.' That is, the road into eternal life is paved with self-immolation: 'Perfection and immortality would not be the lot of the multitude of saved nations until they, too, had undergone death, corporeal resurrection, and life everlasting in the church triumphant' (Smolinski 2000: 39). Indeed, Mede came up with the now-popular notion of a new dispensation, initiated by what would later be called the Rapture. The point is that apocalyptic notions require martyrdom. They are intended to terrify all whose personal attributes and pursuits impede the progress of the millennium and the reign of Christ. Making the apocalyptic a this-worldly dispensation or process leaves the door open for renewed demands for self-mortification.

It is time, therefore, for a thorough-going and collective renunciation of this historically destructive vision of the future. So long as the churches give the aura of legitimacy to apocalyptic beliefs, they not only will be providing reinforcement to those who wish to see just such a collective exorcism: a final conflagration that purifies the nation through the self-immolation of the people. They will also be adding fuel to the fires of teachings and visions that require the self-immolation and self-mortification of the soul.

Turning the apocalyptic vision into a mandate for self-purification in this life also leaves the door open for using the prospect of future cataclysm to terrify those who resist such appeals. For instance, in the

Enoch tradition, the unrighteous are those who 'have not experienced struggle and battle in their lifetime. They have died in glory, and there was no judgment in their lifetime.' That is why their souls must 'experience evil and great tribulation – in darkness, nets, and burning flame.' They have not suffered enough in this life to merit eternal satisfaction. Only those who have persevered in righteousness and who have adhered to the wisdom of this tradition have suffered enough, and only they will finally be set free from the burdens of time. To stand the test of time, one must therefore first go through a sort of hell before entering into the blessed rest and the final triumph.

For the righteous, if they endure their earthly torments and persist in hope, there is not only a future of glory but the delicious satisfactions of retribution: 'for all your tribulations shall be (demanded) for investigation from the (responsible) authorities – from everyone who assisted those who plundered you. Be hopeful, and do not abandon your hope, because there shall be a fire for you; you are about to be making a great rejoicing like the angels of heaven.'[8] However, while anticipating the joys of seeing oneself and one's people survive as others are being eliminated, individuals must curtail their desires, achieve virtue, and pay tribute to those in authority.

Such use of apocalyptic visions to instill the spirit of self-sacrifice is hardly unique to the Christian and Jewish traditions. Ancient Rome was also adept at using apocalyptic visions of a new city to encourage the surrender of the autonomous soul. In Virgil's *Aeneiad*, Zeus explains to a worried Venus the fate of her son, Aeneas: despite his many losses, he will 'establish city walls and a way of life,' a new city that centuries later would become Rome. 'No need to be afraid, Cytherea./Your children's destiny has not been changed./As promised, you shall see Lavinium's walls/And take up, then, amid the stars of heaven/ Great-souled Aeneas' (Virgil, *The Aenead*, Book I, *ll.* 357; 347–350).[9] However, Aeneas merits this destiny only so long as he is self-sacrificial, a 'dedicated man' (Book I, *l.* 411; Fitzgerald 2000: 14).

A soul thus dedicated has no warrant for publicizing his own sorrow. Constantly mourning the loss of his father and of those who fought bravely in the defense of Troy, he nonetheless keeps his grief to himself. Although both he and his men are at the point of despair after sustaining new losses at sea, Aeneas holds before them the promise of the gods, that they will reach Italy and build there a new Trojan kingdom. 'Burdened and sick at heart,/He feigned hope in his look, and inwardly/Contained his anguish ... Aeneas, more than any, secretly/ Mourned for them all' (Book I, *ll.* 284–6; 300–1; Fitzgerald 2000: 10–11). Aeneas is first of all a man of sorrows, acquainted with grief, who can bear the burden of time, and he is therefore fit to be the carrier of the apocalyptic vision and head of a new dynasty.

Apocalyptic visions thus promise to restore the devastated city to its place in history. Hope for a city that will be set on a hill, a city that recalls the glory of Rome, of Athens, or of Jerusalem itself, requires the sacrifice of the soul to the larger society. For centuries, then, the apocalyptic vision has been used to inspire generation after generation of young men to serve Zeus or Father Abraham. The young have come when they were called, especially when, as in the case of suicide bombers, the rewards of heaven are promised to be very swift indeed. Scholars have documented what one calls 'abundant evidence that the fascination with martyrdom and the need to imagine persecution were characteristic of many Christian movements.'[10] It is possible even to speak of 'a veritable thirst for public death and a popular Christian view that would-be martyrs already had one foot in the heavenly world' (Frankfurter 2000: 436). To those who were preparing to be immolated, the secrets of the heavenly world would be opened up in dreams and visions. 'Apocalyptic clairvoyance' was the reward for those who would be willing to deny themselves the satisfactions of this world, including life itself (Frankfurter 2000: 436–7). Like Islam's appeal to submission and self-sacrifice, the churches have long based their appeals to self-sacrifice on an apocalyptic vision of infinite satisfaction.

Apocalyptic beliefs offer the prospect of a final release from all the burdens of selfhood and individuality. That burden is heaviest, of course, when all the familiar or traditional ways of supporting and defining the self are no longer very useful. For instance, when people experience what Kermode calls the 'acceleration of history,' they sense that they are living in unforeseen and unprecedented times, and they begin to realize that they, too, may also be as unique and unprecedented as the world in which they are living. No longer do they see themselves as being merely part of a world that spans the generations and ties the living in close bonds of devotion and familiarity to the dead.

Such a period confronts people with their own temporary and fragile, uncalled-for selves. They have only a self that lacks both a precedent in the past and any foreseeable future in this life or the next. The self, under these conditions, is not only unique and unprecedented; it is also unrepeatable, and its failings can never be reversed. There is no historical warrant and no second chance for the self. Many individuals therefore worry about what will become of themselves and long for posthumous recognition.

Apocalyptic beliefs provide just this reassurance for those who are willing to sacrifice themselves in the meantime. In return for self-immolation, the self is guaranteed posthumous recognition and legitimacy. For instance, in the *Testament of Moses*, presumably written near the turn of the Christian Era, a protagonist, Taxo, has been urging upon himself and his sons that they should all fast together to death in order to precipitate divine retribution on the enemies of Israel: 'There let us die rather than transgress the commandments of the Lord of Lords, the God of our Fathers. For if we do this, and do die, our blood will be avenged before the Lord.'[11]

Short of self-immolation, rituals may relieve individuals of the burden of individuality by providing the comfort of antique and formulaic language, the vestments of memory and tradition, and the assurances of apocalyptic vindication. All of these deny the uniqueness of the individual.[12] Indeed, rituals give individuals a symbolic foretaste of the apocalypse by initiating them into the sacrifice of personal difference. In this way rituals assert the primacy of the social order over the individual. The innermost self remains a mystery to be revealed only on the Last Day to God. To inquire about that mystery is to acquire secret and unauthorized self-knowledge.[13]

Christian orthodoxy typically has been suspicious of individuals who claim to have their own sources of inspiration and authority or who acquire an identity that does not visibly derive from the ecclesiastical storehouse of authorized possibilities. In various visions of Hell, whether enacted in *autos da fe* or in mob lynchings, the churches have occasionally edified the public with little apocalypses: glimpses of the punishment awaiting those who defy ecclesiastical authority or the will of the local community. Similarly, over the last three centuries, puritan and evangelical Christians have used the threat of the Last Judgment to mount a series of attacks on the autonomous soul. Certainly, the evangelical wings of the Protestant churches have long provided excruciating forms of soul-searching, remorse, self-mortification, and they require the repudiation of whatever might seem to be unique or unprecedented about the self. The evangelical's insistence on the disciplines of self-denial and self-mortification, along with their promise of a final exorcism of all differences and of the destruction of all rivals and enemies, derives from medieval Catholic piety a tendency to turn this life into a continuing purgatory of relentless self-purification and self-improvement. This practice may be compared with rites of exorcism in other traditions, for example folk Hinduism.[14]

So long as the apocalyptic imagination is domesticated in ritual and convention, the promised satisfactions remain in the distant future. To prepare for the apocalyptic satisfaction requires prolonged and persistent self-abnegation. In return for self-abnegation over a lifetime, the apocalyptic vision holds out the possibility of a total loss of self, whether in adoration, rapture, or total re-absorption into the cosmos.

While claiming to liberate the individual from an oppressive spirit, these rites in fact impose the standards of the social order on deviant individuals, especially on young women who refuse to be domesticated or on children who claim to have their own sources of inspiration and authority.[15]

Consider the apocalypse, then, as a collective exorcism of the unauthorized and deviant self. Like an exorcism, the apocalypse is expected to reveal and destroy the spiritual forces that long have been at work, hidden below the surfaces of social life or in the depths of the psyche. However, like a collective exorcism, the apocalyptic vision undermines the freedom of the individual spirit to explore and embrace unauthorized ways of living and dying. In the end, in both exorcisms and in the apocalyptic imagination, only the true believers, the orthodox and right-minded, are to be left standing. The last shred of individual difference is finally destroyed. On the final day, the individual is absorbed into a collectivity engaged in continual adoration of the only One who has any remaining claim to uniqueness, authority, and finality.

In the last analysis, even the Christian God abandons any such claim to selfhood. As Thomas Altizer has recently argued, 'modern apocalyptic thinking revolves about the subject of both consciousness and history, but a subject that is here a self-negating and self-emptying subject, and precisely therein a subject which is finally that Subject which Christianity, and perhaps only Christianity, knows as God or Godhead itself.'[16] Thus the requirement of self-immolation is rooted in the nature of the deity.

This deification of self-sacrifice returns us to a consideration of John Donne, with whom this chapter started. Remember John Donne's exhortation to carry out self-destruction for the sake of others less willing to stand up for their beliefs or to give their lives to and for their neighbors. Donne appears to be arguing that the individual who is free to lay down his life for others has achieved a high degree of maturity and autonomy. However, toward the end of the essay (1983: 81) Donne goes further. He argues not only that the act of suicide conforms the individual to the image of God in Christ, but that it obeys a universal 'inclination;' therefore 'men naturally and customarily thought it good to die by self-homicide.'

Certainly, enthusiasts for the apocalypse, like the celebrated flagellants of the thirteenth and fourteenth centuries, have sought through self-punishment to postpone the tribulations of the end, while others have sought by the same self-mortifying means to hasten the Last Day, when old scores would be finally settled (Weber 1999: 55–6). Combining elements of Christian mysticism with a relentlessly ascetic tradition, Donne (1983: 78) argued the case not only for Christian self-mortification, to prepare the soul for the end, but for the active or passive suicide of the Christian: 'Our body is so much our own that we may use it to God's glory, and it is so little our own that when he is pleased to have it we do well in resigning it to him, by whatever officer he accepts it, whether by angel, sickness, persecution, magistrate, or ourselves.' The vision of the end has been turned into a requirement not only for continuous self-mortification but for an active hand in one's own death, when nature or the larger society should demand it. Self-mortification thus lies at the core of apocalyptic belief and practice. Being a Christian therefore entails not only 'simply yielding to death when it comes' but also a willingness to bring about one's own death by holding 'a contempt of this life in respect of charity' (Donne 1983: 84–5).

The apocalyptic vision attacks the psyche by suggesting that to die to oneself is the way to overcome death. At the very least, such self-immolation is a way of exorcizing the past, of paying off old emotional or moral debts, and of beginning a new world, where there are no tears, and where death has no more power. Cast in a more heroic mold, self-mortification is a way of taking on oneself the burden of the community's past and of leading the way into its future. Like Aeneas, who redeems the loss of Troy by fulfilling his father's apocalyptic vision of a new Troy that would extend throughout space and time, the heroic individual loses his own will and bears the burden of time in sure and certain hope of final victory.

To add to their terrifying aspects, apocalyptic visions and doctrine have long extended an invitation to the faithful to die for their heavenly cause. Virgil's vision of a 'dedicated,' 'great-souled' Aeneas is the sort of heroic character that would serve well the imperial interests of Rome under Augustus. Virgil has Zeus go on about the work of Romulus, who 'will take the leadership, build walls of Mars,/and call by his own name his people Romans. For these I set no limits, world or time, But make the gift of empire without end' (Book I, *ll.* 372–4; Fitzgerald 2000: 12). Again, the victory over time is complete, and the validation of Aeneas's sacrifice of himself is not only the permanence of the final settlement, with the renewal of the Trojan kingdom, but the glory of the Roman Empire and its victory over 'subjugated Argos' (Book I, *l.* 384; Fitzgerald 2000: 13). Apocalypses seldom withhold the promise of revenge for old losses and humiliation, but some promise them only to those who, like Aeneas, are willing to undergo perennial self-sacrifice.

Aeneas, 'a man apart, devoted to his mission,' is dedicated to the point of self-immolation. Not only did he endure new losses that re-opened old grief, but he also risked his life, time and again, for the sake of his 'fated future.' His will, then, was not his own but was surrendered to the future as that had been willed by the gods; he has no other life to live, and no soul apart from that mission. This proclivity to self-mortification begins to be understandable, of course, early on in the *Aenead*, as Virgil reminds us that there were times when Aeneas had wished that he could have died, years before: 'Triply lucky, all you men/ To whom death came before your fathers' eyes/Below the wall at Troy! Bravest Danaan,/Diomedes, why could I not go down/When you had wounded me, and lose my life/On Ilium's battlefield?' (Book I, *ll*. 134–9; Fitzgerald 2000: 6–7). Clearly Aeneas is one who would have preferred to have laid down his life for his friends, in obedience to the will of the fathers of Troy. His is a life dedicated to redeeming the original losses of Troy, its city and its men: a living sacrifice by the dedicated man.

The Christian churches learned all too well these lessons in self-immolation for the sake of an apocalyptic vision. In the first centuries of the Christian Era enthusiasm for a martyr's death was so widespread that pagan commentators were amused, and some theologians tried to discourage the faithful from such willful volunteering.[17] Some Christians no doubt admired the Cynics and the Stoics who extolled the benefits of suffering and dying for one's own ideals. They longed for death, and like Tertullian wrote and preached extensively on the virtues of suffering and martyrdom. As fighting is to a soldier, so is suffering to the Christian: an honored way of life, consummated in death (Bowersock 1995: 63).

The apocalyptic vision promises relief from all the burdens of time, including individual singularity, the weight of remembered cataclysm, and the sense of being oppressed by social obligation. In some Christian apocalyptic visions, believers are thus encouraged to look forward to a Day of Rapture, in which their spirits are literally possessed by their savior. In return for this loss of selfhood, the faithful are allowed to witness the destruction of the world from their preferred seats in the Christian gallery, while the rest of humanity is consumed in apocalyptic conflagrations and earthquakes and in the final battles that immediately precede the Christian millennium.

If it were only to prevent any further encouragement of self-destruction, the Christian community should repudiate its apocalyptic legacy. It is inevitably seen as encouraging self-immolation, after a divine model, in order to guarantee a purified selfhood at the end of time. A repudiation of such beliefs is all the more imperative in an age of suicide bombers and of twenty-first-century crusades against various embodiments of 'evil.' Add to these considerations the tendency of apocalyptic beliefs to inspire terror and to legitimate the repetition of past disasters, and it becomes even more clearly incumbent on the Christian churches to discredit the literature that has reinforced and intensified the human impulse to revenge and self-destruction.

Notes

1   John Donne, *Divine Meditations* 13, ll. 1–4; in John Donne, *The Complete English Poems*, edited by A.J. Smith. London, 1986, p. 314.
2   James Moorhead, 'Apocalypticism in Mainstream Protestantism,' in *The Encyclopedia of Apocalypticism*, Vol. 3, *Apocalypticism in the Modern Period and the Contemporary Age*, edited by Stephen J. Stein. New York: Continuum Publishing, 2000, pp. 72–107; p. 81.
3   Donne, *Divine Meditations* 14, ll. 10–14; in Smith (ed.), 1986, pp. 314–15.
4   John Donne, *Suicide*, transcribed and edited by William A. Clebsch. Chico, California: Scholars Press, Studies in the Humanities Series No. 1, 1983, p. 78.
5   Hal Lindsey, with C.C. Carlson, *The Late Great Planet Earth*. Grand Rapids, Mich.: Zondervan Publishing, 1970.
6   Cf. Andrew L. Roth, "Men Wearing Masks": Issues of Description in the Analysis of Ritual,' *Sociological Theory*, Vol. 13, Issue 3 (Nov. 1995): 301–327; see pp. 305, 314.
7   Barry Schwartz, 'Memory as a Cultural System: Abraham Lincoln in World War II,' *American Sociological Review*, Vol. 61, Issue 5 (Oct. 1996): 908–27; see p. 918.
8   I Enoch, 103, 6–8; 104, 3–5; in '1 (Ethiopic Apocalypse of) Enoch (second century BC to first century AD). A New translation and introduction by E. Isaac,' in James H. Charlesworth (ed.), *The Old Testament Pseudepigrapha*, Vol. 1, Garden City, New York: Doubleday, 1983, pp. 5–89; pp. 84–5.
9   *The Aenead*, Virgil, translated by Robert Fitzgerald. New York: Vintage Books (1981) 1990, p. 12. All quotations from *The Aenead* will be from this edition, noted as Fitzgerald 2000.
10   David Frankfurter, 'Early Christian Apocalypticism: Literature and Social World,' in John J. Collins (ed.), *The Encyclopedia of Apocalypticism*, Vol. 1 *The Origins of Apocalypticism in Judaism and Christianity*. New York and London: Continuum Publishing, 2000, pp. 415–53, p. 436.
11   Testament of Moses Ch. 9: 5–7; in J. Priest, 'Testament of Moses,' in James H. Charlesworth (ed.), *The Old Testament Pseudepigrapha*, Vol. I, New York: Doubleday, 1983, pp. 919–34, p. 931.
12   Rituals thus embody what some sociologists have called a 'primary framework,' whose 'existence and meaning precede the event it interprets,' Barry Schwartz, 'Memory as a Cultural System: Abraham Lincoln in World War II,' *American Sociological Review*, Vol. 61, Issue 5 (Oct. 1996): 908–27; see p. 911.
13   Jacques LeGoff, *History and Memory*, translated by Steven Rendall and Elizabeth Claman. New York: Columbia University Press, 1992, p. 89.
14   See Isabelle Nabokov, *Religion Against the Self: An Ethnography of Tamil Rituals*. New York and London: Oxford University Press, 2000.
15   Ibid.
16   Thomas J.J. Altizer, 'Modern Thought and Apocalypticism,' in *The Encyclopedia of Apocalypticism*, Vol. 3, *Apocalypticism in the Modern Period and the Contemporary Age*, edited by Stephen J. Stein. New York: Continuum Publishing, 2000, pp. 325–59; p. 356.
17   In this account I am drawing entirely from G.W. Bowersock, *Martyrdom and Rome*. New York and Cambridge: Cambridge University Press, 1995, pp. 59ff.

CHAPTER 6

Apocalyptic Visions as Ideology

The apocalyptic vision divides the world into two opposing forces, only one of which will prevail in the end. In holding on to this vision, the Christian churches are thus regenerating old hatreds that began with the rivalry of cities and empires in the ancient Near East. Long before the advent of Islam and Christianity, the known world had for several centuries been involved in an ancient contest between East and West: a contest fought between city-states and large empires. Residues of these contests, and of their disastrous consequences for the inhabitants of the cities of the ancient world, still survive in the apocalyptic visions of Islam and Judaism as well as of Christianity. This is the common residue, and it accounts for the convergence of these world religions in the twentieth century toward a single, apocalyptic scenario. These ancient memories disguise themselves as self-fulfilling prophecies of a day of reckoning to come, in which new cities are destroyed to satisfy ancient wrongs. Although one may deplore the contemporary hatreds that have produced the bombing of Baghdad and New York, of Jerusalem and Kabul, neither Christianity nor Islam and Judaism have renounced the apocalyptic culture of relentless determination. Judgment must begin somewhere. That is why I argue that the time is long overdue for the churches to rid themselves of the apocalyptic fantasy of a day yet to come.

The contest between East and West continues today, as names like Vienna and Baghdad are added to the list of places to be destroyed. Certainly, Islamic revolutionary thought in Iran has seen Islam as being caught up in an historical struggle between East and West beginning with the expulsion of Islam from Spain and intensified by the defeat of the Ottomans outside of Vienna. For some Islamic states, the only solution has been 'the emancipation of Iranian culture from Western domination, which involved a relentless attack on intellectuals who were the bearers of Western culture in Iran.'[1] It is the same hope, but in reverse imagery, when Christian extremists long for the day when Christians will be purified of the influence of Babylon, with its Muslims, secular humanists, feminists, and homosexuals.

Still another reason for taking apocalyptic beliefs off the books of Christian orthodoxy is that they are dangerous to the survival of any nation that holds them. Not only do these beliefs justify the wholesale destruction of nations that stand in the way of American sovereignty and of Israel's claims to Palestine; they also interfere with essential reality-testing. Jerry Falwell, on the radical Christian right, prophesied a nuclear war with the Soviet Union early in the 1980s, but he was confident that God would come to rescue the people of America and preserve them from a nuclear holocaust (Lienesch 1993: 229). The Christian right continues to argue for the use of nuclear arms on the grounds that, for the faithful Christian, there can only be eventual rescue and vindication (Lienesch 1993: 228). Similar fantasies assure some right-wing Christians of the nation's final immunity even if military push comes to nuclear shove in the Middle East. Certainly, 'with Israel's founding, affairs in the Middle East took on new eschatological meaning' (Lienesch 1993: 229).

These apocalyptic delusions of immunity derive from the Christian right's belief in the United States as the Christian nation destined to lead the world. America is the new Israel. Like Israel, the United States therefore bears the burden of God's redemptive purposes in history, and it alone will stand the test of time. Thus nothing should stand in the way of the unilateral assertion of American power. Furthermore, the United States should be willing if necessary to go it alone. Indeed, the emphasis of the Bush administration on the unilateral assertion of American power, its contempt for coalitions and the United Nations, and its willingness to contemplate not only pre-emptive strikes against other nations but also the use of nuclear arms, is entirely consistent with the views on American sovereignty held by Pat Robertson and the Christian Coalition. For them, America is the only hope of the world, and on its actions now depends the future and the fate of every nation. Should America fail, the only winners will be Satan and the forces of evil.

Once again, however, it is far too easy to accuse the Christian right of having extreme ideas, when the same convictions are still quite legitimate within the so-called mainstream Protestant and Catholic churches. All of these churches have rituals that confer a virtual innocence on individuals who take the liturgical opportunity to confess their sins and to hear themselves absolved and forgiven. Once admitted into the circle of those who have pleaded guilty to various unspecified charges, they are fit to take part in the symbolic re-enactment of the murder of Jesus Christ. As I have mentioned already, they also are allowed on Good Friday to take the part of the crowd, when it calls for the release of the criminal Barabbas and the crucifixion of Jesus Christ. That is, the ritual implicitly allows them a share in collective guilt for the crucifixion while having certified them as sufficiently innocent to be participants in the liturgical re-enactment of his death. This same combination of overt innocence and implicit guilt is part of many rituals, not the least being those that involve sacrifice: the taking of animal life in exchange for exemptions from divine wrath and punishment.

What is implicit at the level of ritual is explicit in apocalyptic mythology. The vicarious myths of the end-times promise those who are found innocent a certain satisfaction in being able to witness the torment and destruction of those who have been found unworthy to pass the final test. At the very least, to contemplate being among those who are found to be sufficiently innocent before the bar of divine judgment is also to contemplate in advance the satisfying vision of endless torment inflicted on one's former oppressors. The vision gives to those who aspire to innocence an advance showing of this coming attraction of one's detractors being subjected to unspeakable suffering.

It is this same apocalyptic vision, however, that allows individuals and, indeed, whole societies, to undertake violence with a clear conscience. Those are not guilty of violence who inflict it under the mandate of a divine imperative. Take, for example, Baruch Goldstein, the American doctor who became a settler on the West Bank. A follower of the slain rabbi Meir Kahane, Goldstein settled accounts with Islam by shooting to death twenty-nine Muslims, and injured many more as they were saying their prayers in a hall at the Tomb of the Patriarchs. At his funeral, a rabbi announced that Goldstein was innocent: not so, however, those whom he had killed. His victims, after all, were guilty of the deaths of many Israelis in 1929, never mind that many of them were not alive at that prior time. It was Goldstein himself who was innocent, since he had 'acted "for the sake of Jewish honor and to sanctify the Name of Heaven"' (Gorenberg 2000: 205). Like Aeneas, he was a dedicated man whose will was not his own, since he was acting under a divine mandate and seeking to fulfill a heavenly vision of a new community destined to satisfy old longings and to settle ancient scores. As Gorenberg (2000: 247) goes on to point out, success in war breeds a sense of entitlement to further victory and continued domination. I write these words as the United States, having conquered Iraq, is beginning to raise questions about the role of Syria and Iran in providing a safe haven for war criminals as well as for weapons of mass destruction. It is as if the innocence conferred on those who carry out a divine warfare against the forces of evil entitles the victors to impose their will on those who stand in the way of their sacred mission. The wedding of innocence to violence, articulated in apocalyptic myths, is consummated in victorious combat.

Apocalyptic beliefs thus reinforce a dangerous sense of imperial entitlement and of immunity to destruction. Not all America's enemies, however, are alien. For the Moral Majority and the Christian Coalition, evil forces are as ancient and as foreign as Babylon, but they are also as modern and domestic as the secular humanists. Not only are the forces of evil largely to be found in the Middle and Near Eastern nations among the Arabic descendants of Ishmael; they also include 'the people of the Babylonian humanistic and occultic [sic] traditions' who will be opposing 'the people of the Abrahamic, monotheistic tradition.'[2] These are the secular humanists and their occult allies who will 'eliminate the influence of the people of faith' in a new world order led by the United Nations and by the enemies of Israel.[3] The apocalyptic vision of the Christian right sees the country itself as needing to be purified of pernicious influences. Robertson links the likes of Hitler and Genghis Khan with the Council on Foreign Relations and all those liberal academics who are intent on imposing an anti-Christian new world order through the United Nations. Indeed, for Robertson, the Christians, the real Christians of the world, are in the same danger as were the Jews under Hitler. Just as the Nazis used propaganda to alienate Germans from the Jews, so have the establishment and the secular humanists done everything in their power 'to ruin the influence of Christians and their ability to block Satan's plans' (Robertson 1991: 257).

Furthermore, he fears that the United Nations will impose its rule by making Israel leave the West Bank and surrender Jerusalem. Such a move would then issue in the final war between East and West, with Christian forces led into battle by the United States against satanic legions intent on imposing their own version of new world order. To prepare for this battle, Christians and the people of God everywhere must free themselves from the control of secular humanists, homosexuals, adulterers, People for the American Way, and devotees of New Age cults. Once the battle begins, Christians will not have long to wait for the millennium to begin, the Thousand-Year Christian Reich. If for no other reason than that apocalyptic beliefs have nourished the fascist hatreds of the Christian right, the Christian community should divest them of their orthodox status and their place in the canon, once and for all.

Emboldened by their apocalyptic pretensions, the ideologues on the right demand an imminent and fundamental change in the order of things. To delay decisive action, to consult with allies, to subordinate national initiatives to the control of an international body: all these temporizing strategies are untrue to the Christian right's vision of an imminent end. From their ideological viewpoint, pragmatic diplomacy sacrifices what is rightly due to those who have already waited far too long for important positions in the rule of God. Imbued with an apocalyptic vision, they can see no alternative to cosmic battle in a war to end all wars. Those who would temporize, delay, falter, or fall back are the internal enemy. Indeed, Robertson, Jerry Falwell, and their evangelical supporters have done everything in their power to impede any peace initiatives that might require Israel to withdraw from the settlements on the West Bank.[4] Certainly, there is no room in their ideology for those who would surrender land for peace and thus delay the return of Israel to all of its promised land, including the Temple Mount itself.

Apocalyptic beliefs thus give indirect theological legitimacy to ideologies of hatred that demand and justify a final solution. For the apocalyptic imagination, the world is full of antagonisms that can only be resolved by the radical extermination of all who live outside the imagined circle of salvation. Remember that, for Pat Robertson, there are two kinds of people:

> On the one side are the beliefs of a portion of humanity that flowed from Abraham to the Jewish race and to the Christians of the world. These are the people of faith, the people who are part of God's world order. On the other side are the people of Babel–those who build monuments to humanity under the inspiration of Satan. (Robertson 1991: 257)

This latter group deserves extermination.

For the Christian right, it is the humanists and the liberal elites who are the source of pollution: the heirs of Babylon and its occult mysteries, the agents of Satan, the secularists who will 'sell out America' (Robertson 1991: 259). They are thus an advance guard of 'the world government of the new world order' and its primary legions. Like a fifth column, they are subversive and internal to American society: 'the secret planners of the Establishment ... [typified by someone who is] educated at Groton, Harvard, and Oxford, who then goes to work on Wall Street' (Robertson 1991: 259). These are the people who have no knowledge and respect for 'what goes on in the hearts of people in Iowa, Nebraska, Texas, or Florida' (Robertson 1991: 259). They look down on the real Christians as being fundamentalist, bigoted, literal-minded, parochial, anti-modern, conservative, and even reactionary (Robertson 1991: 263). Their pernicious influence should be driven from American society.

Unlike those educated in the halls of Ivy League colleges and universities, the people value 'free enterprise and free speech' and 'intense patriotism' (Robertson 1991: 259). Like the Jews, the conservative Christians are 'the people of faith, the people who are part of God's world order' (Robertson 1991: 257). Therefore all the others are part of the secular world that is always – and already –

passing away. In terms of the apocalyptic imagination, secular humanists are already on death row.

Thus, in preserving their apocalyptic tradition, the churches have continued to provide theological cover for an ideology of simple hatred very much like anti-Semitism. The enemy personifies and desires the destruction of the world in an all-or-nothing conflagration, with the winner surviving among the remnant of the purified and like-minded. Like earlier forms of anti-Semitism, the apocalyptic ideology of the Christian right projects its own hatreds on to the enemy, who therefore seems wholly demonic. Because the time is coming for the Rapture, when Christ will elevate his own for a view of apocalyptic destruction, Christians need another Moses, who will separate the true followers of Christ from the half-hearted believers, the humanists, and the secularizers. It is therefore no accident that Pat Robertson (1991: 237ff.) concludes his book on the new world order with instructions on how Christians should put the major commandments into practice as they prepare for the end.

By retaining the apocalyptic framework of their own beliefs, the Christian churches lend credibility to hopes for eventual triumph over all the rivals and enemies of the faith and of the nation. By keeping alive an apocalyptic orthodoxy, the churches sustain hope for a day when all foreign influences and all deviant forms of devotion will have been destroyed, and the good will be separated once and for all from the evil. Israel, the old one or the new, will be vindicated and revenged, her aggrieved people satisfied at last, as the surviving nations come to offer their tribute at her altars. Islam has the same dream, of foreigners who either convert or offer tribute in return for toleration and protection, and who thus acknowledge the supremacy of Islamic faith. Similarly, the Nazi advocates of a millennial Reich could stand no rival claim either from Jews or, in the end, Christians. The apocalyptic battle and revelation will leave no difference standing.

It is futile for the churches to try to resolve conflict between Islamic and Christian nations when their own Scriptures look forward to a day of triumph over all rival faiths. It is in fact a vision of ethnic cleansing, dressed up as a religious exaltation. In the Middle Ages the apocalyptic imagination envisioned a new emperor or king who would soon mobilize the poor, destroy the rich, and spread wealth among all those who had been starved into hopelessness and submission. This apocalyptic announcement took many forms, not the least of which prophesied the return of an emperor who would humiliate and destroy the Roman Church, disperse and kill the luxurious clergy, dissolve the monasteries and convents, impoverish the burghers and artisans, and introduce the returned emperor's own millennial kingdom. As Norman

Cohn (1970: 118ff.) has argued, this was indeed a German apocalyptic vision, in which the French would be subjected, the Turks driven out of the Holy Land and from Eastern Europe, and the ancient fraternity of all German peoples restored to its original unity and purity. To those familiar with the apocalyptic pretensions of national socialism in Germany during the past century, these medieval aspirations will seem strangely modern.

It is also futile for the churches to deplore the destructive ideology of Nazi Germany, so long as Christians are encouraged to hold the very apocalyptic expectations that have long nourished fascism. There is no doubt that the medieval apocalyptic imagination was nationalist, communist, communitarian, and populist. It was also profoundly anti-Semitic, regarding Adam and his descendants as Germans. In regarding the Chosen People and early Christians as exclusively Germans, it claimed for the German people a sacred history with a unique mission to usher in a millennium of justice, freedom, equality, and national harmony. The Nazi belief in a millennial Reich was therefore an ancient Christian heresy used in the end to bolster the faith of a nation near total collapse.

This is not the first time, then, that the churches have used apocalyptic beliefs to shore up their declining community or nation. Consider New England in the mid-seventeenth century. During the early stages of that colony's struggle for survival, apocalyptic imagery gave the Massachusetts colony a much-needed ideological claim on the lives and loyalties of the new settlers. Back in England, Cromwell seemed to be bringing the reign of the Catholic monarchy, and thus of the Antichrist, to an end. Attracted by this apocalyptic scenario, a large number of settlers had begun to head for home. To stem the tide of returning settlers, it was necessary to give the struggling colony a rival apocalyptic attraction. A number of clerics obliged by developing an apocalyptic theology to define the colonial situation.[5] In Massachusetts, for instance, John Eliot (1604–1690) proclaimed the Indian population to be the lost tribes of Israel (Smolinski 2000: 46–7). In order to fulfill apocalyptic prophecies of the return and conversion of Israel, he subjected the Native Americans to the same disciplines of study and prayer, belief and behavior that were incumbent on the colonists themselves, and he succeeded in creating several communities of Christianized Native Americans. In this way, the colonial periphery in America continued to defend itself against the magic of the English center.

Apocalyptic ideology was not limited, however, to the cultural defence against the appeal of the homeland. The frontier itself underwent conflict with the Native Americans that soon threatened the survival of the entire colony. Thus a soldier in the Massachusetts militia proclaimed the times ripe for the overthrow of the Antichrist and called for the sacrificial death, if necessary, of Christian soldiers (Smolinski 2000: 47). Jonathan Edwards, who felt that the apocalypse had already begun during the Reformation, and that the days of the Antichrist were therefore already waning, still regarded the people of God as caught up in a cosmic battle against Satanic forces: 'the Antichristian kingdom (the beast), the Mahometan kingdom (the false prophet), and the heathen kingdom (the dragon)' (Smolinski 2000: 58).

Americans have thus used apocalyptic ideology not only to attract loyalty away from the homeland to these shores, but also to turn hatred and aggression away from themselves on to the Native American population. George Washington in 1779 ordered Major General John Sullivan 'to lay waste all the settlements around ... that the country may not be merely *overrun* but *destroyed*' (in Berlet and Lyons 2000: 26). Thus 'the Revolution deflected popular aspirations away from the possibility of radical land reform and focused on the supposedly empty land to the west' (Berlet and Lyons 2000: 26). As the poorer farmers went west into land formerly claimed by France and still under its influence, 'the French and then the British were placed in an apocalyptic and millennial framework by insurgent colonists,' who saw the Catholic Church and finally the British themselves as the incarnations of the Antichrist (Berlet and Lyons 2000: 25). The time had come for a battle with the enemy that would leave the land in the sole possession of the faithful people of God, with the land finally purified of every enemy. Thus apocalyptic ideologies shore up nations when their identity or even their survival is at stake.

If these ideologies are now enjoying renewed currency, it may be because some foresee the end of their civilization's supremacy. Pat Buchanan (2002: 256) worries that:

> the time of the West has come, as it does for every civilization, that the Death of the West is ordained, and that there is no sense prescribing new drugs or recommending painful new treatments, for the patient is dying and nothing can be done. Absent a revival of faith or a great awakening, Western men and women may simply live out their lives until they are so few they do not matter.

Clearly, this apocalyptic view is intended to be a self-defeating prophecy. Those who read it are being called into a renewal of commitment to the Christianity that has made the United States great: a new commitment to the faith of the fathers.

Buchanan argues that the nation is facing two threats. One is coming from the immigration of peoples who have no reverence for the American past and no willingness to sacrifice themselves for its future. The other threat is far more deadly, because it comes from within the nation itself. Buchanan's *bêtes noires* are the feminists and environmentalists, the cultured despisers of American history and the ethnic polemicists who scoff at the nation's ideals. If the nation forgets its original vision, it will become another casualty of self-doubt and of rancorous self-hatred. Unable to transcend its own violent history and the heavy casualties of both the civil and world wars, the nation may lose heart altogether. America is being destroyed from within by the young people who are most forgetful and the critics who are most contemptuous of the faith of the forefathers. What worries Buchanan is that the nation may not stand the test of time.

Buchanan is writing to shore up a nation-state whose internal dissensions may have sapped its will to live and now threaten to undermine its continued purchase on space and time. Buchanan (2002: 256) announces that 'America needs men and women of more kidney, spleen, and heart if the struggle for the soul of America is not to be irretrievably lost.' In the meantime, the vision of Washington and the Adamses, of Madison and Jefferson, is not only being ignored but dishonored, and the heroic sacrifices of those both in the South and the North who gave their lives for their nation are dishonored and forgotten.

The United States has long borrowed its moral capital from the churches' treasury of apocalyptic merit. Until the churches discard their apocalyptic dreams of glory, they will guarantee the legitimacy of the apocalyptic imagination, not only in the polity but in American culture itself. In the nineteenth century, Moorhead (2000: 76–9) argues, preachers proclaimed that the time had already begun when the kingdoms of this earth would be transformed gradually into the Kingdoms of God. The coming Kingdom could be found in such secular developments as the improvement of the conditions under which people were living and in the spread of people and ideas through innovations in transportation and communications. These were the signs that the apocalyptic age was emerging continually, perennially, in the mundane as well as in the extraordinary: not only when the soul of the individual came face to face with the judgment of God. It was therefore 'plausible to invest secular changes with positive religious meaning and to use traditional eschatological symbols to depict a future in which sacred and profane forces would advance in harmony, a future over which the saints would enjoy mastery' (Moorhead 2000: 78). However, no one knows better than Moorhead himself that this apocalyptic vision of a progressive unfolding of the Kingdom of God is now regressing to Buchanan's far more beleaguered and even paranoid view of the danger in which the nation stands.

In fact, the claim of the United States to being the new Israel predisposes the country to feel beleaguered by foreign influences and by internal dissent. It is essential to the apocalyptic vision to view the nation as being in distress. During the first half of the first century CE, Israel's culture was actually infiltrated by gentile notions, and its sovereignty was being subordinated to Rome. Herod the Great, who became a member of the imperial household, had brought Roman and Hellenistic sports and theatre to Jerusalem, had peopled the hinterland with cities open to gentiles (the Decapolis), and had established in Caesarea Maritime a cultic shrine to the goddess of Roma, whose statue stood alongside that of Augustus in honor of the imperial cult. Prophets like Ezekiel had long identified such foreign alignments with prostitution because, as Yarbro Collins (2000: 399) has argued, 'Tributary alliances between Israel and other nations had long been seen as involving "some recognition of the foreign religious symbolic system and thus of their deities ..." The cult of Roma is a good example of the inseparability of the religious and the political in antiquity' (Yarbro Collins 2000: 399). So is the cult of Israel, old and new.

Clearly Israel was running out of time even before the destruction of the city of Jerusalem in the conflagrations of the civil war. Its cultural boundaries had been eroded by the Hellenization of its communities and their customs. Israel's monarchy had become an extension of the imperial household. After the death of Herod the Great, some of its territory was administered directly from Rome, and the remainder was turned over to client kings from Herod's family: Jewish kings, but from a dynasty of questionable legitimacy. Not only was the royal dynasty compromised and interrupted by conflict between the generations, but the young men in the larger society were spoiling for a fight: eager to remove emblems of Roman hegemony from the gates of the Temple, to prevent any intrusion of Roman insignia into the country, and finally to cease once and for all the prayers offered in the Temple on behalf of the emperor. It is therefore not surprising that the churches' apocalyptic beliefs reflect Israel's early and deep suspicion of foreign influences.

For the churches to maintain these beliefs, however, is to perpetuate Israel's beleaguered view of its social universe. In holding on to the apocalyptic beliefs that promised the people of Israel a day of triumph, restoration, and return, the Christian churches continue to enshrine the turmoil of this period, just as surely as Islam has enshrined the memory of the sufferings of the Prophet, his cousin and son in law, and of Fatimah herself (Ayoub 1978: 198–9). No wonder they are popular with

Protestants who decry foreign immigrants and the erosion of the cultural purity of an earlier age.

The churches' use of apocalyptic visions to demonize the enemy embodies Israel's fear of foreign influences. To mingle their own prayers and devotions with those directed on behalf of the emperor was to flirt with the danger of infidelity, prostitution, and bestiality. Not only could the goddess Roma be portrayed as an elegant prostitute, but the power of Rome herself could be identified with the beasts and dragons long familiar to the Near Eastern apocalyptic imagination. To be sure, that portrayal of the goddess of Roma as a prostitute, or as a 'luxury-loving woman of loose morals,' also reflected outrage over the destruction of Jerusalem. However, the same beliefs also served to deter Christians from offering deference to Rome and its institutions (Yarbro Collins 2000: 400). They now serve to enflame the Christian right's fear of international engagements.

The image of the Whore of Babylon (Rev. Ch. 17) riding on a beast has long stirred the apocalyptic imagination to find new terms of ideological abuse (Boxall 2001).[6] Ideologues for the Church, from Jerome onwards, have found in the lady on the beast the epitome of all the world's seductive allurements, distraction, and stimulation: an ink blot for the patriarchal imagination to construe as it will. Consider Morgan Beatus, who in the tenth century 'portrays Babylon in Oriental garb, reclining on a divan, with the crescent moon on her headdress, almost certainly reflecting contemporary conflicts between the church of Christ and Islam in medieval Spain' (Boxall 2001: 61). Used by the Christian right in the United States, the Whore now stands for those who threaten the treasures of the Christian tradition. Thus when Pat Robertson and others see secular beliefs and values or Islam as the very image of the Whore of Babylon, they join a long tradition of those who used apocalyptic visions to foment a paranoiac fear of alien and domestic rivals.

If the future is ever to hold out promise for a world no longer at war with itself, apocalypticism must no longer provide the format for sacred history. No longer do Christians need to predicate their own survival or vindication on a day of apocalyptic glory. Indeed, such expectations threaten their survival and increasingly rob them of any chance of being vindicated before the bar of humane opinion. The churches have an opportunity to discard their vindictive literature, with its poisonous apocalypticism, before it is too late to stop the enthusiasts of the Last Days from having their way.

Notes

1 Mansoor Moaddel, 'Ideology as Episodic Discourse: The Case of the Iranian Revolution,' *American Sociological Review*, Vol. 57, Issue 3 (June 1992): 353–79; see pp. 364–5.
2 Pat Robertson, *The New World Order*. Dallas, London, Vancouver, Melbourne: Word Publishing, 1991, p. 258.
3 Ibid.
4 Gershom Gorenberg, *The End of Days: Fundamentalism and the Struggle for the Temple Mount*. New York, Oxford: Oxford University Press, 2000, pp. 157–69.
5 In this account I am following closely the argument of Reiner Smolinski, 'Apocalypticism in Colonial North America,' in *The Encyclopedia of Apocalypticism*, Vol. 3, *Apocalypticism in the Modern Period and the Contemporary Age*, edited by Stephen J. Stein. New York: Continuum Publishing, 2000, pp. 36–71.
6 Ian Boxall, 'The Many Faces of Babylon the Great: *Wirkunggescghicte* and the Interpretation of Revelation 17,' in Steven Moyise (ed.), *Studies in the Book of Revelation*. Edinburgh and New York: T&T Clark, 2001.

CHAPTER 7

The Test of Time

In times of war, of course, and especially after a serious defeat, societies are in a position to leave the past behind, and they face an extraordinary set of possibilities that they would not otherwise have been able even to consider. Germany, after having started and, finally, having been defeated in the First World War, faced just such a situation. It was one in which the defeated could have acknowledged their loss without bemoaning the past or the future, while confronting the victors with their responsibilities for the future of that nation. Rather than engage in such direct negotiations, however, the leader of the Bavarian republic, Kurt Eisner, took a more dramatic, even tragic and romantic, view of the passage of time. David Runciman puts it this way:

> His mission as he saw it was to cleanse the political life of Germany, starting in Bavaria, by embracing the idea of German war-guilt. In Eisner's world, everything that preceded November 1918 was immoral, sinful and corrupt; everything after could be beautiful, healthy and pure, if only German politicians would own up to the wickedness of what had gone before.[1]

Note the language of corruption and purification. It suggests that, after its defeat, what Germany needed was a national exorcism: a dramatic way of completing and correcting the past and of initiating a future unlike any that had gone before or yet been imagined. It is precisely such rhetoric that distinguishes the apocalyptic imagination, and it is also just such an imagination that gives fascism its spurious moral force. Not incidentally, it was also in Bavaria that the fascist movement under Hitler made its strongest gains: the politics of purification leading to a demand for a new, millennial Reich.

Since Kurt Eisner was more interested in the politics of morality than in the means by which good intentions could be translated into reasonable consequences he avoided going to Paris, where the Versailles Treaty was being discussed, or to Weimar, where the new constitution was being formed, but went instead to a fruitless congress of international socialists in Berne. In Paris he could have taken the defeat as a matter of fact and confronted his victors with their responsibilities for the future of the Germany that had just been destroyed, and in Weimar he could have contributed to the formation of a new constitution for the German Republic. Instead, he preferred national self-flagellation for the past and dreams of a purified future that would never come. In so doing, he became the very model of the religious politician Max Weber despised: moralistic, unrealistic, self-serving, and irresponsible (Runciman 2003b: 6–7).

It is indeed difficult for any society to graduate from the past into the future, since the very identity of a society requires a sense of continuity over time. The presence of a constitution that permits or even requires a process of constant revision and innovation may give the illusion of continuity while in fact promoting changes in the social system itself. It may even succeed in subjecting all its arrangements, including its most fundamental institutions, to continuous review and revision to prepare for contingencies that have been imagined but not yet arisen. Such a future, however, remains contingent on actions taken on the basis of precedents and procedures agreed upon in the past.

As for the past, a secularizing society may require itself to take full responsibility for bringing to light all outstanding grievances, as in the South Africa that finally emerged under the leadership of Nelson Mandela. However, such a process does not create a firewall that protects the present from the eruption of old passions and longings for national contrition and purification.

Modern societies are thus caught between two alternative scenarios. One requires gestures of national contrition and purification that overcome the past and initiate a dramatically new future. The other requires a process of temporizing based on precedents for reaching decisions and a willingness to undertake a process of continuous and incremental rather than drastic change. The character that is required for the first alternative to be acted out on a national scale is religious, perhaps profoundly so, but in ways that Max Weber, with perhaps Kurt Eisner in mind, famously despised. Weber preferred politicians with an ethic of responsibility: an ethic that made them peculiarly aware of the consequences of their own actions and inclined them to hold others, even their conquerors, accountable for theirs (Runciman 2003b: 6).This latter sort of character would be capable of taking a nation through a process of continuous changes, none of them based on dramatic repudiations of the past or on grandiose gestures of introducing the future. Instead, the very model of a secular politician would be someone who took the passage of time seriously enough to dispense with any imaginary attempts to transcend it. Instead, the secular politician would take full responsibility for all the consequences of any action or policy and would prefer to be judged by results than by intentions. He knows, as Runciman (2003b: 6) puts it, that:

the best intentions will generate unintended consequences, and the
mark of a responsible politician is how these are dealt with. The
way to deal with them is to take responsibility for them, which
means neither denying them nor wallowing in them, but accepting
them for what they are: the unintended but foreseeable consequences of any involvement in politics.

'Stuff happens,' the American Secretary of Defense's notorious remark
about the United States' responsibility for the catastrophic looting of
Baghdad, is not what Weber had in mind.

To understand the social character necessary for the development of a
secular society, then, it is necessary to grasp what it would mean to live
without dreams of religious or, for that matter, any other kind of glory.
In Weber's view, such a character would lack all the qualifications of the
charismatic leader. It is the charismatic character, in fact, and popular
longings for charismatic leadership that stand in the way of the
development of truly secular societies. Charisma, Weber argued, holds
the passage of time in contempt. That is why charismatic characters are
not interested in careers, in which their achievements over time would be
the basis on which they would be judged. Indifferent to consequences,
they are adept at making the sort of claims that cannot easily be put to
the test of time. That is why they ignore details and remain above the
concerns of the mundane and the everyday: concerns for what they shall
eat or drink, or for what the morrow might bring. They leave such
concerns to their followers, who are more or less enchanted by the
charismatics' visions of personal and national transformation. Even
charismatic leaders, however, must stand the test of time. In the long
run, and sometimes in the short one, their followers will demand results.
Despite their claims to stand above the passage of time, charismatic
politicians, even those who claim to be the recipients of a special grace
from their Lord and Savior, will be judged on whether their followers'
lives have been measurably improved. Not even leaders of the Christian
right are immune from the test of time.

What social character would be required that would be free of the
charismatic demand for a final, apocalyptic time in which a society will
be free of its past and, purified by suffering and contrition, ready for a
more glorious future? Is there a social character imbued with a sense of
its own validity and vitality: able to confront a past that has hitherto
been ignored or denied, and able to live without hopes for an
apocalyptic resolution of all suffering, faults, and ambiguity? What
institution or practice would prepare the way for such a social character:
to create the sort of person able to enter into a moment or event fully
aware that it is a new and unprecedented situation, unique and

unrepeatable, and able to act with the knowledge that any such action will have unintended consequences that will never be reversible. Such a character would be able to act without adequate foreknowledge while taking full responsibility for the outcome.

Weber's preference for the social character of the Protestant workman does not begin to go far enough. Granted that Weber is right about the Protestant ethic of responsibility. The Protestant artisan does take time seriously, works punctually, gets results, and pays off his or her debts on time. However, such a character has long been criticized for missing the moment and for mortgaging the present to the future in the name of an antiquated ideal of virtue or virtuosity.

Injunctions to this-worldly asceticism have long been countered with popular nostrums to live in the present. Even these countercultural protests, however, have failed to grasp that any moment, if you enter into it deeply enough, may well be filled with a past that comes back unexpectedly and finds a people unprepared to satisfy its long-standing but often suppressed demands. The experience of time cannot be reduced to an ethic or character that refuses to bemoan the past or takes full responsibility for the consequences of actions undertaken in the present without adequate knowledge of the future.

There is what might be called a 'fall into time.' Many individuals also live reasonably happy and successful lives, and yet wonder if they have somehow missed the boat. The appeal of 'the road less taken' is widespread. Many individuals, perhaps most, reach a point in their lives when they wonder what they might have done or who they might have become had they only taken another course earlier in their lives. Rather than remaining so preoccupied with their careers, they could have followed their impulses to become an artist or a politician or a doctor, or to know their children and serve their spouses. Thus the past comes back to haunt the present with a sense of unfulfilled possibility.

Thus the apocalyptic vision may appeal to those who feel they have a debt of unsatisfied love or animosity or with an unfulfilled potential. Those who cannot wait for the end to come for their tears to be wiped away may also yearn for a release from the burden of time. Are there institutions or social practices that would be able to cultivate a social character that is not subject to these yearnings for apocalyptic fulfillment and final judgment? Certainly, there are religious communities that require their adherents to come to terms with a past that indicts them both for what they have done and also for what they have not done: for the persons they have been, in secret, and for the persons they have failed to become.

Confessions and absolutions offer an acquired but temporary immunity to the passage of time by requiring small revelations of the individual's past and symbolically clearing the way for an authorized future. However, these medicinal doses of apocalyptic transformation must be repeated over a lifetime in order to exempt the individual from being exposed to an unrepeatable and irreversible encounter with time. Death is symbolically transcended, and the individual need therefore never graduate into an unimaginable future. It is ironic that the churches have been unable to create a social character capable of an unmediated and direct experience of the passage of time, despite a Gospel story about One who indeed suffered from such exposure. Indeed, I will return to the question of the Gospel story in the last chapter.

Here I am simply suggesting that it may be very difficult, regardless of the churches' halfway measures, to develop a social character that is inured to – and even welcomes – the passage of time without romantic hopes for the future or dramatic gestures toward redeeming the past. The psyche itself may be traumatized by the encounter with time. Consider, for instance, the familiar 'examination dream.' There are many versions of this dream, but a fairly common one goes something like this.

It is late in the academic year. Suddenly you realize that the time has come for you to take an examination in a certain course. However, you had forgotten that you were enrolled in that course, and so you have not attended classes in it or done the assigned reading. The past, of which, until that moment, you had been happily unaware, breaks into your conscious state in the dream, and you suddenly realize that there are things you have left undone that you ought to have done, and there is perhaps something you have done, like enroll in that course, that you should not have done. As you begin to search for the room where the examination is to be held, you become increasingly anxious. Even while you are still trying to make up for lost time, you know it is already too late. You are responsible for failing something you did not know you had ever undertaken, and there is no remedy for your flaw.

In the dream you suddenly realize that you will not graduate, and that all these years in which you have claimed to be a graduate, you have been living a lie. No wonder that you may wake up from the dream with enormous relief that you have actually earned your degree and that you graduated long ago. If the dream haunted you with the sense that you are not the person you thought you were, on awakening you realize that you are that person, after all. If the dream tormented you with the sense that you were a case of arrested development, you know, on awakening, that you have indeed grown up. If the dream reminded you that in some sense you have never left your foster mother, your alma mater, when you awake you realize that after all you have left that original environment and are now on your own. You have stood the test of time.

Thus the dream confronts individuals with their failure to pass the test of time. Although they may have thought that they had indeed passed that test, that they had earned their degree and graduated from their alma maters, they have not done so. The dreaded future, in which they have nothing to show for the time they have spent, no indelible markers of their existence, still lies before them.

Like the apocalyptic vision, the dream reveals a future that one would have gone to any lengths to avoid: a future in which one has failed to pass the test of time. No wonder that religious institutions offer so many opportunities to pass that test, along with assurances of final vindication and of a delayed graduation into a world beyond the passage of time itself.

In the same way, the examination dream therefore reminds people of a past they have long felt it safe to ignore. Many carry forward into their later lives, into their work and their new families, the passions and rivalries which they first experienced in their childhood family settings. The family romance goes on, and childhood yearnings, loves and hatreds, can be brought forward and directed not only toward a new family but to friends and co-workers alike. At least in the unconscious, we do not leave home completely, and we find ourselves therefore going forward into a past from which we had long thought we had graduated. Because out-dated hurts and longings persist, there is always unexamined work to be finished.

In the formation of a secular social character capable of engaging the passage of time with few defenses or allusions, then, more is needed than a religious ethic of responsibility. More is needed than the rites and practices that give individuals limited engagements with the past and the future. More is needed than a plethora of therapies that seek to help individuals heal from the inevitable traumas of time: the lost opportunities, unassuaged grievances, and the illusions of an unexamined maturity. There is some untold agony that may never be alleviated by language. When individuals split off a particularly sad or hungry part of themselves, they no longer have to feel its anguish directly. Instead, the split-off part of the self begins to die and sends messages to the psyche that it is running out of time. The psyche may then take the message personally, as if it is the individual herself that is failing a crucial examination and may never get out alive. Thus the trauma of time may come from a deeply embedded part of the self, suffering from solitary psychic confinement.

When agony remains suppressed and untold, individuals are at a loss for words to let anyone know of the trouble they have seen. Like the voice in the African-American spiritual, the only one who knows their trouble is a God whose suffering stands for theirs in some way, beyond the reach and understanding of ordinary mortals. Closed off in a mental space of their own construction, what was once the vital part of their souls is dying slowly of isolation, just as surely as does a prisoner in solitary confinement. Time is indeed running out on the soul that is repressed, confined, shut off from consciousness, and unable to tell its story to those who will both believe and fully understand.

To deprive such souls of apocalyptic hope may seem cruel, especially since the only future they can anticipate is one that has no organic connection with the present, but seems to burst into the present as though from another world of experience and possibility. The passage of time is taking them farther from their true selfhood and closer to their own expiration date. Time-running-out thus becomes the symbol and substitute for the lost soul. No wonder that so many long for more time, whether to take a final test and so to graduate from the past, or to recover an old friend or lover whose presence could make one feel whole again: vital and alive to a world of possibility.

There are many other reasons why individuals may find that the passage of time is unbearably slow and burdensome. Their lives may be blighted as those whom they love sicken and die, or they may be trapped in relationships that are frustrating or demeaning. Failure in work, living in a community that is in decline, the loss of one's social standing, indeed rejection of any kind, isolation and retirement: such a list is virtually endless even before we consider the internal, psychological processes that go by the name of depression. Individuals who are in fact mourning the loss of themselves live a shadowy existence. They are shadows of their former selves, no matter how energetic they may try to be or the extremes to which they go to feel alive once again. They may seem shadowy, not altogether real, to other people as well, who find their company disconcerting because it suggests not the presence of another human being but their absence. For the terminally ill, the imprisoned, or those suffering a decline in their mental faculties, the present may weigh especially heavily and yet feel empty. Their cry, like that of the sufferers in the apocalyptic vision of John, is 'How long?'

The question is whether there is an institution or a social practice that could train individuals for secularity by providing non-toxic or even therapeutic exposure to the passage of time. How may individuals be trained to satisfy long-neglected longings and pay forgotten debts, to reveal secret sins and give voice to untold agony, to cope with the unique and unprecedented, and to face a test for which individuals and communities, not to mention whole societies, can never be fully prepared? How may individuals be prepared to initiate a future which may well not turn out to be the one they intended, but from which there will be no escape? Such a practice or institution would allow the future to begin because the past has been completed, but it is a future for which there would be no useful precedent and perhaps no remedy. Even a people's sacred history would be of little use in defining the times in which they would be living and there would be no prospect of reversing the consequences of prior actions.

Certainly, the Christian Eucharist is intended to provide precisely these challenges and satisfactions. In the confession one repents of what one has done and not done, of sins that one can remember and those that are long forgotten. One also remembers a moment which was then and still remains both unique and unprecedented: the death of the son of God. One faces a judgment from which no amount of repentance or praise can provide a certain immunity, and in the sacrament itself one enters into a future that promises, for those who receive the sacrament rightly, the joys of heaven; for those who receive it unworthily, it is the beginning of a long and terrible end.

However, such liturgical victories of ritual over time are temporary and have to be repeated. No rite can provide for the complete satisfaction of repressed longings, guarantee relief from a past that one has long ignored or forgotten, present a moment that is in itself unique and unprecedented, or enable participants to enter into a future that remains as imminent as it is opaque. For Christians, the Eucharist is given over and over again precisely because the moment that it provides is inherently insufficient. It does not matter how often the celebrant proclaims that the Eucharist remembers an act, the self-offering of the son of God on the cross for the sins of mankind, that was in itself unique and unrepeatable. Still the Eucharist itself must continue to be repeated, Sunday after Sunday, year in and year out, over time, until the last feast is given, in which the celebrant is the son of God himself, and the company is the living and the dead from both earth and heaven.

Of course, no ritual can adequately simulate the test of time. Consider rites of exorcism that offer mini-apocalypses: revelations of untold agony, an opportunity to lift the burdens of the past, a chance to settle old scores, and a unique, unrepeatable opportunity to rid the future of the past. In fact, however, because these rites attribute the sufferer's anguish to a departed spirit or to a demon, they offer sufferers only a surrogate voice and a highly mediated experience of selfhood, whose results may simply perpetuate the past and return the individual to a way of life that is unsatisfying or oppressive. For instance, the anthropologist Isabel Nabokov tells of a young South Indian couple who were 'poor, sick, and demoralized.'[2] The husband, Mahentiran, had reason to be depressed. His younger sister had died early in her

adolescence, and he himself was failing at selling fruit. To compound his
resentment, his older brother was successfully monopolizing a much
more advantageous location for such a business. Mahentiran developed
headaches, and it became increasingly difficult for him to support his
wife and two small children. In the midst of these difficulties, his wife,
Rita, dreamed that her husband's dead sister had appeared to offer
protection for the family if only they would do her the honor of
worship. The couple consulted a medium, who conjured up the spirit of
the dead sister and gave voice to the sister's dissatisfaction with the
attention she had been receiving since her death. The medium burst into
funereal lamentations and wails, and the couple themselves began at last
to weep. As Nabokov goes on to suggest, 'The very onset of these dirges
forces everyone within earshot to surrender to the moment: none can
resist the mood of bottomless sorrow they impart. The wails inevitably
induce weeping all around' (Nabokov 2000: 122).

Such a moment does allow the grief-stricken to experience their
sorrows through the mediation of a spirit, with whose unhappiness they
deeply empathize. Thus the moment offers an indirect expression of
personal agony through a surrogate self, the medium.

However, such rites offer only a partial and temporary relief from
untold anguish and a chance to grieve: a reprieve from irreversible loss
while old loves have a chance to breathe. This interim period can go on
indefinitely for those who depend on communion with the departed to
soften the pains of separation and loss. For the troubled South Indian
couple who discovered the source of their difficulties in the unfulfilled
longings of the husband's dead sister, the ritual of exorcism provided an
occasion for mourning but did not lead to a final separation between the
living and the dead. The couple continued to live as if their lives were
engaged in prolonged waiting for a time that might never come. While
the rite helped them finally to acknowledge their own longings for the
departed and to give them at least a temporary fulfillment of their
unspoken affections, it perpetuated a moribund relationship between
the living and the dead. The ritual, although it allowed room for the
release of pent-up emotion, literally enshrined the dead in the hearts of
the living by requiring that a shrine be erected in the home.

Such a rite does not really offer a chance to pass the test of time;
there is no graduation from the past into the future, and no way to
finish a course that has been undertaken but not yet completed. On
the contrary, the husband, Mahentiran, discovered that the dead are
part of life in the present and that he himself is part of a society that
transcends the passage of time. No matter how desperate his
circumstances are, and no matter how it may seem to him that he
has no future, he is now able to participate in a time that transcends

that of his own sorrow. Nabokov points out that a community's sense of its own place in time is being played out here, as if the dead and the past are 'here and now, there and then, everywhere and everywhen, altogether.' Thus nothing is forever lost: no time, no love, no person. In return for acquiring partial release from the weight of unexpressed grief, the couple continued to live under the spell of the dead and of the community that has the power to bring the past into communion with the present. There is no graduation from the community and the presence of the dead.

Granted that there is some value in the cathartic weeping that was released in the course of the rite, we must nevertheless wonder whether such a rite is more like the disease than the cure. The 'disease' is simply that the living have no way to experience themselves as being real, substantial, and fully present because their affections and identity are so closely tied with the dead. Unable to grieve completely, they may seem to be only a shadow of their former selves. They lack presence if only because their hearts are 'somewhere else,' and they are unable to live fully in the present. Their affections are moribund because they are still invested in the dead. It is as if they embody the person who is now gone. In the more extreme instances of protracted grief, it is as if there has been a fusion of souls between the living and dead: a close identification that may have begun many years before the loss of the one who was so deeply loved. What is needed is to recover the soul of the living from its affections for the dead.

Thus some rituals provide a medicinal dose of apocalyptic revelation at a fairly high price. On the one hand, there is a recovery of the past, a re-opening of the graves to allow the dead a voice in the community, a rekindling of old affections between the living and the dead, and the revelation of emotions that have been suppressed. Individuals do acquire a past that comes to them as something of a surprise. In the example of the grieving South Indian couple, they discover that they had undertaken a course of mourning for the husband's dead sister: a course that they had never finished.

However, such a ritual fails to confront individuals or a community with the full impact of the unique, the unprecedented, and the irreversible. The future never begins. In the Christian Eucharist, for example, such a moment is remembered and re-enacted rather than allowed to happen in the present. Indeed, what does happen in the present is a highly formalized act subject to chronic repetition. Although such a rite may open up hidden aspects of the past, may bring the dead back into communion with the living, and may confront individuals with aspects of their past that they have not fully recognized or worked through, it nevertheless allows them to avoid taking an irreversible step into the future. Such a rite is like a symptom: a compromise with the passage of time.

It is very hard to let go of a past that one does not know that one has. The psychoanalytic project is to free the individual of the past enough to make it possible to enter the future unencumbered by unnecessary emotional burdens. To get rid of guilt for crimes one has not committed and of longings that are inherently hopeless is good preparation for a future which is attractive and dangerous enough on its own terms. First, however, it is crucial to know and to put into words what it is about the past that one has not fully acknowledged. Interestingly, some of the marriage rites observed by Nabokov enable the spirits of deceased relatives to articulate their resentments and fears, which are uncannily close to the more or less conscious but unacknowledged feelings of those about to be married. The past comes back briefly to haunt the new couple as they prepare for the future to begin.

More is needed to articulate the unacknowledged past than for spirits to provide a moment of psychodrama. As individuals enter new relationships or abandon old ones, they do face what for them is unprecedented and unrepeatable. The step they are taking may also be irreversible, as in the case of parting with the dead, although many individuals may seek to postpone or reverse this departure by seeking to maintain contact with the dead. It is understandable if they take a number of backward steps toward a more secure and promising period of their lives. Underlying some of the conversation between the living and the dead is a yearning, on the part of the living, for an emotional union with the figures in the past whom they thought would nourish and protect them. The coming of the departed spirits of the parents to live with the couple is simply the outward and visible sign of an inward longing for emotional fusion. This ancient merger is an aspect of the past that is seldom consciously remembered or articulated, although individuals may talk easily of protected relationships in their lives as symbolic replacements for the womb. The longing goes deeper than metaphor, and the body, at least, remembers a time when it did not have to worry about the future. On the cusp of the moment between past and future, individuals may take emotional steps backward to a past for which they still unwittingly yearn.

Like the examination dream, rituals reveal how difficult it is for the psyche to take the test of time. That test means not only the revelation of hidden attachments to the past but an encounter with something unprecedented, in the present, and an irreversible step into what has now become the future. These, indeed, are the rudiments of the apocalypse. Whether they occur in dreams or are found in rituals that reveal a past that had remained a mystery, they plunge one into a new situation where one encounters a future containing long forgotten challenges. One may have thought they had graduated, left home, relinquished an old love or hatred, or buried the dead, but in the examination dream, as in many a rite, these prior departures seem to lie ahead.

Even rites that seem to require individuals to take an irreversible step into the future recycle aspects of the past. For instance, Christian marriage rites ask a couple to leave their families of origin behind, to make promises, and to enter the future not as two persons but as a couple united in the bonds of matrimony. However, the same rite offers reassurances that such a step is neither unique nor unprecedented but an institution 'ordained by God' and blessed by the Son of God many hundreds of years before. In stepping into the future, they are entering into a situation prepared for them long in advance, and they are doing so in conformity with long-established rules and procedures. Even when divorce is widely practiced and accepted, it is clear that the step into marriage is irreversible; the bonds may be broken, but short of an annulment one cannot return to a period in one's life before that marriage has taken place. Divorced is not the same as never-married. Indeed, the social and psychological effects of the marriage may last long after the final separation, although the bond may be broken.

It is therefore not surprising that marriage rites seek to place the irreversible act of marrying into a longer time-frame: to attenuate that moment and thus make the intensification of time more bearable. Consider marriage rites in South India. There, when individuals get married, they no doubt undertake a step that, for them, is unprecedented, but the rite itself also marries them to the past. For instance, Nabokov (2000: 125ff.) shows how brides are inducted into an order of women that reaches well back into the very distant past: 'What is wanted is a generic human bridge between the generations: a bride, a woman who will reproduce the past in the present' (Nabokov 2000: 133). In a ritual that invokes the father or mother of the groom and places them in the new household, the link with the past is established in 'a "marriage" between the living and the dead' (Nabokov 2000: 136). It is a marriage, once again, that solemnizes the control of the community over the individual and of the social order over the woman, who is thenceforth intended and expected to embody the ideal wife rather than to have a life and identity of her own.

Note how such a rite cautions the wife against an assertion of her selfhood. The ritual specialists often conjure up a spirit whose identity is at first in doubt, who is not entirely willing to go through with the ceremony, and who may not be 'willing to subordinate his/her individual identity to the larger set of relationships that constituted the family' (Nabokov 2000: 132). In this way, the wife, whose identity is henceforth to be submerged in the family as she takes on the role of the ideal wife, may hear her own inner doubts and misgivings being portrayed. However, the rite allows her only the substitute satisfaction of symbolic self-assertion before she is inducted into a life of self-less devotion. The spirit can voice despair over losing her self in marriage: not the bride. In the end, the spirits of the dead relative no longer struggle for autonomy but 'selflessly devote themselves to perpetuate the family' (Nabokov 2000: 135). The mini-apocalypse of the ritual does reveal the otherwise unspoken agony of the woman whose identity is about to be submerged in a new family, and it initiates the very future which the spirit apparently is seeking to avoid.

Can we say of these rituals that they inure the individual to the passage of time? Do they create a social character that can indeed discover what they have ignored or buried in the past, enter into an unprecedented situation, and take steps that are as unrepeatable as they are irreversible? The rituals we have considered here are deeply anchored in both space and time; they do follow ancient precedent. Moreover, they provide only a simulation of events that bring the past into the present, reveal ancient wrongs, and cry out for the redress of old grievances. The prime actors in these rites are surrogates for the individuals who are actually becoming married or getting exorcized. The individuals themselves are subordinated to the larger play in which they are bit actors. While reminding individuals that they are taking steps that, for themselves, are unique and unprecedented, they are only going where others have gone before, and they are acting not alone but in consort with the spirits of the past. Even graduation ceremonies follow a traditional pattern and frame the rite of passage itself within the collective memory of the academic institution and of the community of scholars.

Perhaps no institution can make the past come alive, articulate old longings, reveal what has been the hidden agony of a people, and precipitate the future without framing such events in a collective narrative that assimilates the new to the old, the unprecedented to the ancient. That is, after all, in the nature of an institution: to provide a continuing temporal framework even for the most innovative of activities. However, we are still left with our question of whether any institution or social practice is able to shape a social character that can enter the passage of time on its own terms. This is a wholly secular character: engaged neither in nostalgic and remorseful reminiscence nor seeking to keep the past from being opened to examination. This individual is able to take the test of time knowing that he or she is not fully prepared and may indeed fail to graduate. However, this secular character does not reduce the uncertainties of the moment to the terms of ancient oracles and predictions. The answers to his or her questions are not written even in sacred texts. However, this secular soul is also able to face the future knowing that it brings precisely what he or she has been seeking for a lifetime to avoid. Departures for which one was not ready in the past may well lie yet ahead. For everyone, of course, there is one examination for which they will always be late.

Notes

1   David Runciman, 'The Politics of Good Intentions,' *London Review of Books*, Vol. 25, Number 9, 8 May 2003, pp. 3, 6–8, 12.
2   Isabelle Nabokov, *Religion Against the Self: An Ethnography of Tamil Rituals*. New York and London: Oxford University Press, 2000, p. 116.

CHAPTER 8

The Theater and the Courtroom

How, then, may a secular social character ever be formed, if the institutions that do the forming are dedicated to making the new into a replica of the old? How can such a social character develop in rites that allow the individual only a surrogate experience of the self and reduce the future to a fulfillment of ancient obligations? If not in ritual, could it be that in the theater individuals may find their own apprehensions about the passage of time voiced not by departed spirits but by characters who have returned from a mythic past? It would be as if the oracles and the dead were allowed to appear in person on stage, and in their presence the actors and the audience could indeed find their own voices, tell of their own agony, and choose on their own terms to enter a future for which there is indeed no adequate precedent. When the curtain goes up or is pulled to the side, there will be revelations of a past long ignored or buried. However, when the curtain goes down and the actors leave the stage, every soul will indeed make his or her own departure. One's time on stage or in the play will indeed have expired, and yet one lives.

Moreover, the theater offers more degrees of freedom than an institution like marriage and the rites that we have considered in the previous chapter. The outcome of a play, for instance, may be known in advance, but, as the climax is reached, it may still come with a frisson of surprise or even horror to the audience. The very pulling back of the curtain announces that there will be elements of revelation here, and in many tragedies it is the past that begins to unfold in the present: its secrets at last being revealed. In this process the central figures of the play may discover that they have a past of which they had until the critical moment been wholly unaware, and the very future from which they had long believed themselves exempt now becomes their fate.

In Sophocles' first play about Oedipus, *Oedipus Rex*, the hero finds himself in what is truly, for him, a unique and unprecedented situation. Although an oracle once had prophesied that he would kill his father and marry his mother, he had hitherto believed that he had escaped that fate. True, he once had killed a man at a crossroads, but that man had been a stranger to him: not the man who had raised him from infancy, whom he had always thought to be his father. Besides, the stranger at the crossroads had raised his arm as if to strike him a blow, and Oedipus had responded in self-defense. Similarly, Oedipus had long thought he had escaped the oracle's promise that he would marry his mother. Certainly, the woman to whom he was married and by whom he had fathered several children was not the woman who had raised him from infancy, whom he knew to be his mother.

Thus, as the play progresses, Oedipus recovers an unknown past that had been his all along. Certainly, Oedipus' past is not what he remembers. The parents he had taken to be his natural father and mother were in fact his step-parents, as he learns from the shepherds who had found him as an infant, lying exposed to the elements on a mountainside. These shepherds had saved him and had given him to the man and woman who then raised him faithfully. These were the people whom Oedipus had long known and loved as his true father and mother. When Oedipus hears of the death of Polybdorus, the man whom he had long taken to be his father, he suddenly finds himself relieved of the weight of the prophecy that he would kill his father. Instead of being murdered by his son, Polybdorus has died of natural causes. The dreaded future has been relegated to the world of false prophecy.

However, further testimony recalls to him a scene at a crossroads, where in self-defense he had struck a man who was attacking him: a man who was indeed his father, although Oedipus of course had had no way of recognizing him. Thus Oedipus becomes guilty of a crime of which he had long held himself to be quite innocent. Another prophecy also turns out to have been quite literally true: that he would marry his mother. His wife Jocasta, now revealed as his mother, kills herself. Having been unable to see his true situation over so many fateful years, he faces the unbearable prospect of a future from which until then he had had every reason to believe himself exempt: the future not of a king but of an enemy of the people, an impure being, destined for permanent exile rather than for a hallowed place in collective memory. The dreaded future, his inevitable departure, has become the world of foregone conclusion. The apocalypse has begun, with its revelations from the past, the intrusion of the unprecedented and unrepeatable, and the taking of a step that, being irreversible, marks the beginning of the end. The final revelation of Jocasta hanging from a rope and of a horribly disfigured king heading for death in exile immerses the audience itself into the passage of time. The characters' departure heralds their own.

The experience of time available to the audience is somewhat more immediate than the experience of time in the rituals we have discussed. The characters speak of their own agony rather than having their conflicts voiced by a departed spirit. The secrets of the past are revealed for all to see, rather than being mediated to the faithful by those authorized to interpret the tradition or by shamans who are able to translate messages from the dead. Whereas it takes a priest to re-enact the death of Jesus on the cross, or a shaman to conjure a dead spirit whose grievances remain unsatisfied until the living mourn her properly, there is no other mediation than that provided by the theater itself.

The play itself is less firmly anchored in space and time than a sacred rite, and it may be performed at times and in places of the dramatists' choosing. The events, unique and unprecedented as they are, are taking place in the time of the play itself. Thus, as in a ritual, the past is being re-enacted, and an event is taking place within the time-frame of the performance itself. However, the actors are no longer being acted on by the spirits through the agency of a mediator. They have become the prime actors engaged with the past and the future in a present that is directly available to the audience as well as to the actors themselves. When the audience gains a glimpse of the figure of Jocasta, hanging from a rope, the audience and the actors experience together the perennially unexpected and unimaginable, even though they have long been familiar with the story itself. As Oedipus leaves the stage and walks into solitary exile, the future has begun.

When the theater acts as a courtroom, someone's history is being revealed, his or her relative guilt or innocence construed, and the future is being determined. Thus a play may achieve something of the immediacy of a real test of time, but the framework of the play is 'once upon a time' rather than in the actual day of its performance. There has already been a loss of immediacy as the curtain goes up, and a new time and space are thus unveiled. It is therefore not surprising that, in an effort to achieve a higher degree of immediacy, the play itself simulates the proceedings of a trial.

Indeed, Shakespeare's *Measure for Measure* does precisely that, and the proceedings are apocalyptic indeed. The Duke returns, no longer in disguise, and confronts several guilty parties with a past they did not know that they had had. For instance, Angelo, the Duke's deputy, did not know that he had actually slept with his betrothed, Mariana, instead of with Isabel, who is the object of his current desires. Indeed, Angelo's love for Mariana had diminished when he had realized the actual size of her dowry. Now he must fulfill his promises to Mariana, endow her with his own wealth, and seek to live up to her very real virtues rather than to continue to pretend to virtues of his own. The future for him begins immediately, and it is precisely the one from which he had thought himself to be exempt.

It is clear that Shakespeare's penchant for concluding a play with a moment of this sort derives from the Greek theater, in which a play often concluded with apocalyptic revelations of past injuries, with the speaking of hitherto untold agony, in a moment that is in itself both unprecedented and irreversible: so much so that the future begins as the play itself comes to an end. As we have just seen, in Sophocles' first play about Oedipus the hero comes to believe that he is guilty of crimes he had been oblivious to having committed. However, quite the opposite happens in Sophocles' later play, *Oedipus at Colonus*. There Oedipus comes to the conclusion that, while he had indeed killed a man who later was discovered to have been his father, he himself was not guilty of murder. He had acted entirely in self-defense, and under the law of the times he was therefore quite innocent of any such crime. As for having married a woman who later turned out to have been his mother, he also was not guilty, the marriage having been performed entirely according to the laws of the state. In this latter play Oedipus articulates his own prior agony, his remorse for these acts, and the sorrows of a life in exile, relieved as it was by the love and companionship of his daughter. He does not need others to tell him of his past, on which subject he has become the sole authority. Oedipus now speaks for himself and acts autonomously as the judge in his own case.

Here, on the Greek stage, five hundred years before the time of the Christian movement, revelations of betrayal, transgression, and judgment all have their own apocalypse, and a soul is realized who is able to stand before his own tribunal and to project a life for himself beyond both the grave and the reach of social obligation. Oedipus has become his own prosecutor and defense attorney, his own jury and judge.

Because the last judgment is beginning under his own auspices, Oedipus has no need for others to mediate for him. Stepping across a sacred threshold into a sanctuary dedicated to the goddesses of the underworld, he enters the future. The sacrificial victim, the exiled king whose departure had removed from Thebes the source of that city's fatal pollution, now enters the sacred grove of the goddesses of the underworld, his own priest and mediator. Arranging for the libations to these goddesses on his own behalf, he may now enter their territory with impunity. His action reverses his earlier exile and sacrifice. Having stood the test of time, he is about to graduate: a free spirit, beyond debt or obligation, able to come and go as he pleases, bearing in his own person the shape of the future. Now Oedipus has a will of his own, is his own priest, and walks where only the gods and their mediators hitherto have been allowed to tread. He has presence and represents the freedom to associate himself even with the gods of the underworld.

This is the secular fulfillment of the apocalyptic vision. Oedipus' life did attain a final revelation, in which he pronounces his own unprecedented and irreversible judgment, and enters a future beyond the grasp of social obligations based even on hallowed precedent. Such a day can and will come to those who are the judge in their own cases, who take their lives into their own hands, and who inaugurate their own future. On that day, the individual is free to associate to all aspects of the past, present, and future, and to associate with whatever sovereigns and deities he may choose to honor.

Thus the empty tomb, long before the advent of Christianity, had been a symbol of the time when the actor finally tells his own story, not through the words of an oracle, but in his own way. The buried truths about his alleged crimes, the hidden past, come to light, and he pronounces in effect an absolution on himself. For a soul thus liberated from the oppression of the community and the weight of the past, the future begins. In the end, he heads for his death as a free spirit, who will not be contained in a tomb and will never again be the object of public recrimination or veneration.

Sophocles has Oedipus claim that his grave will never be found in Theban soil. He will not act as a mediator between his people and their gods, or seek to confer any benefit on them. Whatever rites may be performed at his graveside will provide no one with access to him or protect them from the force of his spirit. His tomb, wherever it may be located, will be empty: his soul free to be wherever he wills himself to be. Having reconstructed his past, he now allows himself to be present at no others' bidding but his own. Under the auspices of such a spirit there is no need to wait for a final apocalypse, a last day of unprecedented and irreversible judgment, at some time in a future that remains beyond the grasp of the human calculation.

In this second play about Oedipus, then, Sophocles creates the possibility of a continuing secular apocalypse. It calls for living out a continuing present that consummates the past and inaugurates the future. In the first play, *Oedipus Rex*, Oedipus suffers from an event so far beyond the range of the ordinary that it is virtually unthinkable and unimaginable. So unique and unprecedented, so horrific and yet irreversible, it requires great dramatization if one is even to imagine it, let alone experience it without being overwhelmed. That is why tragedy, writes Jacqueline De Romilly (1968: 5–6) always tries to represent 'one great event, which overthrows all that existed before: it means death, destruction, reversal of fortune; its strength rests on a contrast between before and after; and the deeper the contrast, the more tragic the event.' That is indeed the test of time.

Earlier in this book I have argued that just such a test may have been posed by the destruction of the city-state of antiquity. That city indeed was a world in which people could live and move and have their own being. When it was destroyed, people lost their own place in time. The past could no longer be carried forward through institutions and traditions, or honored in festival and rite. Part of the tragedy was just this loss of the past, which was sundered from the present. The future, no longer guaranteed in sacred promise or imagined through oracle and prophecy, became immanent and yet opaque. Such events were indeed tragic because they exposed the individual and the community to the terror of time without warning and with no relief in sight. All that was left was the passage of time itself: time without any sense of continuity or control from one moment to the next. Anything could and often did happen anywhere at any time.

To be so fully exposed to the unique and unprecedented, the irreversible and unforeseeable, can paralyze the psyche, may sap the will to live and leave the individual open not only to terror but to crippling despair. Under these conditions it is understandable, at the very least, and perhaps essential, that communities and societies once again link the present with the past. Thus in some Greek tragedies the present is seen as a critical moment in which old injustices and injuries come back to haunt the living and to demand both satisfaction and revenge, at the same moment that a long-dreaded future is about to arrive, or indeed may already have begun. So also the apocalyptic imagination construed a day when old scores would be settled, a day of unprecedented punishment and possibility, when for some the long-dreaded future would at last begin, while others, all outstanding differences having been settled, may enter a future that is exempt from the passage of time.

The theater, I have been suggesting, provided a partially secularized form of this apocalyptic scenario and could shape souls partially weathered by their encounter with time. In some Greek tragedies, for example the *Agamemnon* of Aeschylus, the present crisis no longer seems unprecedented but has long been foreseen; the present is simply the time in which the past comes back with a vengeance (Romilly 1968: 14–15). Similarly, in such tragedies the future is not really opaque; rather the nature of the impending tragedy has long been revealed through oracular prophecy. Other dramas come closer to re-enacting the intensity and uncertainty of a tragic event and plunge the hero into fateful choices, the outcome of which always remains to be seen. For Sophocles, oracles may have prophesied the tragic present as the time in which the future was finally to have begun, but the oracle is cryptic about the future of the present, which remains opaque and depends on the outcome of the hero's ability to stand the test of time (cf. Romilly 1968: 16–17).

In Greek tragedy, then, it was sometimes possible to soften the impact of a cataclysmic event by imagining that it was foreseen and that the future is therefore imaginable. The flow of time remains continuous, even though its stream bears away the hero in its fatal current. It is thus already too late for the hero to change its course, but at least some of the terror of time has been assuaged by assuring the audience that time retains its dreadful continuity. The unique turns out not only to have been prefigured but even to have a dreadful precedent, such as in the fall of Troy. Thus the destruction of the city-state itself, which seems to separate the present from both the past and the future, has its own place in time. Too late though it is to prevent or undo the disastrous event, tragedy links it firmly with the past and enabled audiences to enter into it as if into a descent into Hell. There time goes on even if it is too late for the present ever to be freed from the past, and the long-foretold Day of Judgment has already begun and continues without end.

The legacy of heroic tragedy is a descent into Hell for every one who has the will and the heart to make the journey. This descent into Hell constitutes the apocalypse understood as a journey into the depths of the present, where both the past is unveiled and the future foreshadowed. Those who undertake this journey may expect to bear the brunt of the moment, with all of its longings brought forward from the past, and with all the immediacy of the future that is immanent in the journey itself. Thus the apocalypse is no longer a dreaded day in the future but a continuing event in the present, into which not only the heroic but the 'ordinary' may enter. In their descent into time, people are able finally to confront the past, to listen to the voices of untold agony, to hear laments and unfulfilled longings demanding their impossible satisfaction in the present before it becomes too late.

It is in terms of such a descent into time that we are to understand Oedipus' life and its fulfillment in *Oedipus at Colonus*. As we have mentioned, the play takes place at the threshold of a sanctuary dedicated to the goddesses of the underworld. It is to that point that Oedipus' journey has long been tending, as though it were a continuous descent and has reached at last the edge of the infernal precincts. Once Oedipus is ready to part with the past, to relinquish all claims on it for satisfaction and restitution, and has declared himself free of its remaining judgments, he crosses the threshold into the sanctuary itself to pay his respects to the powers of the underworld. That gesture completes the meaning of Oedipus' life as a descent into Hell, in which he has borne the entire weight of a past, been punished for crimes that he did but also did not commit, and has borne the burden of his people's unhappy confrontations with the powers of death.

In *Oedipus at Colonus*, it is Oedipus' rivals and enemies who are still trapped in the past. Oedipus once again confronts his old enemy at Thebes, Creon, but he is rescued in time by Theseus, King of Athens, who goes on to recover Oedipus' daughters and to confront his sons, still fighting a fratricidal civil war over the succession to the throne of Thebes. Their past continues into the present, but it no longer binds Oedipus, who makes his final oblations to the deities of the underworld. Having completed his lifelong descent into time, he leaves behind only an empty tomb.

If in the contemporary Anglo-American experience there is a milieu that shapes a secular character capable of standing the test of time, I would argue that it is less the theater than the courtroom. Although plays may still achieve more immediacy than a ritual, they offer considerably less in the way of an unmediated test of time than does a trial. In the courtroom, as in the theater or in ritual, the past is conjured up. Instead of the spirits of the dead speaking through their authorized representatives, however, or instead of characters returning from a mythic or narrative past through the agency of actors playing their parts, the accused, the eyewitnesses, and sometimes the defendants themselves testify in their own words about what they know to be 'the case.' The only mediation is that supplied by the courtroom itself, and lawyers, unlike playwrights, are not allowed to put words in the mouths of witnesses, who must speak for themselves. Indeed, any suggestion that they are not speaking autonomously, or that their words have been given them by interested parties, is enough to discredit them entirely. The same concerns apply to the jury, whose deliberations must be free from any form of interference by outside parties, and who must come to the trial free of preconceived opinions about the case.

For the accused, the past that opens up before them may be one that they have denied or suppressed, or the past that is ascribed to them may be a fiction imposed by false witnesses. As the past is being re-presented in the courtroom, the jury hears it, as though they themselves are in the presence of a past that is still being revealed, contested, construed, and in the end, determined by the proceedings of the court. Thus the courtroom achieves a new level of immediacy for all participants: a higher level of direct engagement with the passage of time. The past is defined when the verdict is given, and when the sentence is pronounced, the future starts immediately. It is time itself that is being constructed here, and the actors themselves face the test of time before the bar of justice.

Even the courtroom, however, is unable to dispense with precedent. Indeed, in order for the law to be applied to a new situation, it is always necessary to shape and constrain the actors' accounts so that they will evoke the very precedents that the advocates have in mind. Witnesses need to be able to convince the jurors or the judge that their own testimony is really the case, but it is only on the basis of precedent that the jury or the judge will know whether it is a case, for instance, of negligence rather than of premeditated injury.

Furthermore, although the future begins when the trial is concluded, the proceedings themselves may have been flawed in some way and may not pass the test of time. The sentence may be appealed, the past revised in another trial, and a new future created for all concerned. There is far more uncertainty and indeterminacy in the course of a trial and in its aftermath than on the stage. The judicial test of time may be inconclusive, and, for the parties to the trial, their graduation into the future may be postponed to an as yet uncertain date. Furthermore, in many cases, defendants are encouraged by their advocates to plead guilty to a lesser crime than the one of which they are accused, although they are indeed innocent, in order to avoid the lengthy and costly proceedings of a full-scale trial by jury. Thus the institution of the law itself may inhibit the discovery of what is in fact unique, but which could only be discovered to be unprecedented during the course of a lengthy examination before the court. That is why, of course, the actions of few trials are permitted to be irreversible, since the proceedings themselves may not stand the test of time, especially when the courtroom has been turned into a theater, and the lines of the actors have been scripted for them in such a way as to prevent the past from being revealed or a dreaded future actually begun.

What, then, are we to conclude about the possibility that either the theater or the courtroom may yet provide the tests of time that can be formative for the secular social character? Like the much later Virgil who attends Dante's descent into Hell, Sophocles concerns himself with the formation of souls that can stand the test of time. Thus, in Sophocles' later play, *Oedipus at Colonus*, Oedipus comes to the conclusion that, while he had indeed killed a man who later was discovered to have been his father, he himself was not guilty of murder. He had acted entirely in self-defense, and under the law of the times he was therefore quite innocent of any such crime. As for having married a woman who later turned out to have been his mother, he also was not guilty, the marriage having been performed entirely according to the laws of the state. Now at last Oedipus articulates his own prior agony, his remorse for these acts, and the sorrows of a life in exile, partially relieved, as they had been, by the love and companionship of his daughter. He does not need others to tell him of his past, of which subject he has become the sole judge. Oedipus now speaks for himself and acts autonomously in his own case.

If the unconscious does mature over time and is exposed to a series of revelations about the past, it may change its propensities to avoid the test of time. Some individuals may reach a point at which they do not need to be tested and examined, who have indeed finished their own courses, and who have graduated into a future of their own choosing. They no longer need to be afraid of a past that they have suppressed or ignored; they have paid their dues to the passions of infancy and childhood and no longer feel guilty for crimes they never actually committed. Thus they no longer need to fear further revelations, although they do accept responsibility for the choices they have made and for the opportunities they have missed. Toward the end of their lives they may still imagine themselves to be students, and they may still dream that they have lost track of the courses in which they have enrolled, but in their dreams it may still be early in the semester, and they have time to prepare. What they are preparing for, however, is the real test of time: death itself. In their dreams they may be facing graduation, but it is into the graveyard and the repository of collective memory.

What Sophocles dramatizes over the course of two plays about Oedipus is the capacity of the person to stand the test of time: that is, to bring the past and the future into a decisive present. That openness not only entails a full appreciation of whatever the environment, then and now or in the future, might have to offer in the way of threats or opportunities, surprises and disappointments. It also means being fully aware of how one can determine one's own response to these influences and possibilities, whether by entering into and suffering or enjoying them to the fullest extent, or by rejecting them and departing. Much of that required openness, of course, exposes the individual to his or her own internal landscape of emotion and memory. Thus one enters into the present fully equipped with the capacity to feel invitation and rejection, desire and repulsion, opportunity and danger, without confusing the past with the present. In the same way this immediacy enables the individual to understand how much of the future may be at stake in the present, for better or for worse, and thus to enter into an engagement with others with an appropriate amount of apprehension and positive anticipation.

If this sounds like a recipe for burdening the present with the full weight of the past and the future, it is. Under the auspices of the Greek drama, the individual could enter into this radical exposure to the possibilities of the present, and of the past and future as they impinge on the moment, with a certain playfulness. In *Oedipus at Colonus*, however, individuals are reminded of the possibility that they are burdened with guilt for crimes that they have not in fact committed. Certainly, those Athenians who watched Sophocles' drama about the fate of Oedipus were able to be engaged and perhaps even healed through the spectacle of vicarious suffering and liberation. However, they were not as subsumed in the performance as the actors are who are being subjected to an exorcism or who are being married under the eye and in the presence of ancestral spirits who wish to become part of the new household. It is an open question as to what extent the Greek audience was taking part in a ritual or attending a play. The Greek tragedy is perhaps more able than ritual itself to provide an experience in which individuals can distinguish themselves from their roles, if only by having the opportunity to be in an audience watching actors. The theater may have provided a context in which individuals could know themselves over and above any or all of their roles and thus choose what sentiments and memories, hopes and fears, they would entertain: all this without the mediation of a higher authority to tell them what they can and cannot say or do.

To have this self-awareness, of an inner self that is not involved in any performance, is just what the members of an audience bring to bear on the theater. To watch the implosion of the past and the future on the present moment is entirely difficult enough, and to engage oneself in experiencing, however vicariously, the openness and autonomy of the actors as they finally come to own and control their own passage through time is a demanding exercise of the human spirit. However, it is in just such an experience that the self becomes aware of an inner life that is not caught up in any performance. The audience may realize that their own souls are not so easily dramatized, that their inward selves escape public view and enjoy neither the threat nor the blessings of such recognition. Thus the boundary separating healing ritual from public theater is a difficult one to draw, especially in the context of classical Greek tragedy. I would argue, however, that the Greek audience brought enough in the way of active listening and participation to performances of *Oedipus Rex* or *Oedipus at Colonus* to have vicariously experienced the burden of a past coming back to haunt the hero in the present, as well as being able vicariously to anticipate the liberation of a soul that can finally absolve itself of ancient and illusory guilt and embrace the future on its own terms.

Conversely, when individuals do become subsumed by their roles, they become wholly the creatures of social expectations. That is, they lose any distance that might protect them either from the judgments of others or, more dangerously, from the force of their own consciences. The soul indeed can be crushed by any inquisition, especially when the force of those judgments is compounded by an internal sense of guilt. In what has passed for evangelical renewals in the USA, for instance, individuals have been required to take responsibility for the sins of their past, as though their entire, eternal future were hanging in the balance of the confessions and contrition of the moment. Under these conditions, individuals have been known to lose heart and begin to waste away, even to the point of death. The invitation to die, of course, comes in many forms, and those who are forced to retire, who are rejected by society in one form or another, abandoned by a spouse, or required to enter the limbo of a nursing home in their old age: all these are particularly prone to the crushing of the spirit that can hasten the day of death.

CHAPTER 9

Free Association

Many would strongly prefer to keep the apocalyptic vision of a test of time that will come in the latter days, when all outstanding grievances will be aired and settled, once and for all. The longing for such a settlement may account for some of the perennial popularity of books such as the Revelation of John. Its promise that 'God will wipe away every tear from their eyes' (Revelation 7:17) has long sustained many generations through one loss after another, through days of patient and impatient waiting, and in the face of setbacks that seemed to give the victory only to the unrighteous. How is it possible to give up a book that has given countless thousands of Christians the chance to sing in performances of Handel's Messiah: 'Amen! Blessing and glory and wisdom ...' along with the apocalyptic host, in praise to the Lamb before the throne (Revelation 7:12). Without that vision of final ecstasy, who will be able to promise those who have suffered terrible injustice that there will come a day when all their tears will be wiped away: a day when God will 'judge and avenge' their blood 'upon the inhabitants of the earth' (Revelation 6:10)?

Many have taken refuge in the apocalyptic vision precisely because they can not wait much longer to be revived; they are dying slowly, from the inside out. The longer they wait, the more desperate they become. Their cry echoes the lament in the apocalyptic vision of John the Divine, 'How long shall it be, O Lord of all, before Thou shalt judge and avenge our blood upon the inhabitants of the earth.' We know from Martin Luther King's *Letter from Birmingham Jail* that African-Americans have been told for far too long that they must wait, while in the meantime every fresh delay intensifies the memory of past humiliation. However, the cry 'How long ...?' comes from many quarters, and if the churches are to dispense with apocalyptic visions of triumph and revenge they will have to offer something else, something better, in its place. They will have to be able to make promises of release to people who are losing their battles with various forms of oppression and addiction, who lost their way and perhaps their souls, and who long for a time when they will again experience ecstasy and adoration and feel themselves to be fully, and at last, alive.

If apocalyptic literature is increasingly popular, it may be partly because so many people feel as if they have become estranged from themselves, living among relative strangers, and unable to find the way home. For some, life itself is like a bad dream in which one is in a foreign land, trying to catch a plane home to one's own country, but one has lost one's wallet with the tickets. It is as if there were no way to recover a self that has been lost for too long. For them, the apocalyptic vision may be a hope of last resort for a time when their endurance and suffering will be rewarded, and as God wipes away their tears, they will find themselves in the company of a vast throng of people whose suffering has been replaced with ecstasy. Singing in unison with the faithful whose time of trial is finished, they are no longer voiceless or alone.

No doubt the apocalyptic vision appeals to people who are closed off from the wealth of inner resources that alone can make one's life seem to be filled with a wide range of vital possibilities. Although they may take drugs or drink alcohol to recover a momentary sense of vitality, for the most part their lives seem to be devoid of possibility. The secrets that need to be told, the graves that need to be opened, stand for the aspects of their lives that remain painfully rooted in the past. The future therefore seems like an extension of a present without meaning or joy. Time hangs very heavily on their hands, and there is no end in sight, other than the one they may impose on themselves through acts of self-destruction in a desperate attempt to feel once again in control.

Such a test of time is at the heart of the apocalyptic vision: 'Because you have obeyed my call to patient endurance I will keep you safe from the hour of trial which is to come upon the whole world, to test all who live upon the earth' (Revelation 3:11). At the final trial, individuals do indeed face an appalling test. They must be confronted with the secrets of their own past that have been left buried and unacknowledged. They must endure the discovery of a past about which they have long kept silent and that perhaps has become even a secret to themselves. It is a trial in which the past catches up with them, and therefore the test of time begins before they are ready for it.

Is there an institution or social practice that can provide a functional alternative to the comforts as well as to the terrors of the apocalyptic mythology: a way of life or practice that enables the individual to enter fully into the passage of time, into the strangeness of the moment, knowing that it is critical for the past and decisive for the future, without the promise of vindication or revenge? By definition, social institutions are based on precedent. They have their own rules, like those of the courtroom or the theater, by which they construe the present in terms of the past and open situations to a future that is relatively well defined in terms of guilt or innocence, punishment or, for Oedipus at least, spiritual freedom. The individual graduates, having undergone Anaximander's 'assessment of time.' However, the social practice and institution have borne the brunt of time for the individual by mediating between the present and the past. Untold agony is given voice, but only through carefully scripted plays or through the practiced mediation of lawyers. The actors hear their stories being told, whether by spirits or by other actors playing their parts for them on the stage. Some are permitted to speak for themselves, while others must have their stories told for them. One's own past is thus revealed through the testimony of strangers, and what was alien or strange becomes finally familiar. Individuals find themselves in unique and unrepeatable situations, forced to make decisions that will be irreversible, only because their past is being revealed to them by oracles and shepherds, spirits and shamans. The truth of one's own past is revealed, and one's own future determined, by testimony over which one has no control. That is why Sophocles' second play about Oedipus is particularly important for our question whether there is a way in which the individual can stand the test of time on his or her own terms. Oedipus, in preparing for his own death, changes the verdict on his past from guilt to responsibility. He thus drives a moral wedge between his intentions and their consequences, while claiming for himself the right to make his own peace with the goddesses of the underworld. He defines the past and enters the future on his own terms and through his own agency. In the end, Oedipus sustains the pressure of the past and the future on the present without recourse to mediation and without waiting for a sentence from some tribunal or from public opinion. In this chapter, by way of pointing forward to a discussion that lies beyond the limits of this book, I will turn briefly to a consideration of the way that the Gospel writers framed the stories of Jesus. There are two frames, one in which Jesus is an exemplar of heroic engagement with the passage of time, like Oedipus in his old age as well as in his sacrificial kingship. The other frame portrays Jesus as an actor in a much larger apocalyptic narrative, to which he contributes his own life and death and predicts the final cataclysm. If the churches derive their own commissions from the former of these two frameworks for understanding the life of Jesus, they will have no need for the second, which still defines the mandate for the Christian right and sets the stage for national crusades against the forces of evil as well as for the oppression of domestic freedoms and dissent.

The Greek theater, and in particular the legacy of Sophocles' portrayal of Oedipus, may well have influenced the Gospels' accounts of Jesus' life as a descent into Hell, which began with his temptation by Satan and concluded with his empty tomb. In his death, his spirit was free to roam and to become present at times and places that would be beyond the control of any priesthood or popular devotion. He, too, was portrayed as a virtuoso of time: open to the past, entirely free from obligation to Mosaic precedent, and responsive to the needs of the moment and to demands for compassionate action. For the future, too, Jesus was reported to have displayed a similar openness and autonomy: his Spirit would come, but only at times and places beyond others' control.

I am suggesting that the Gospels' accounts of Jesus carry forward the search for an exemplar of temporal heroism: for someone who can stand the test of time. As an ideal type, this hero would live as though the apocalypse were a continuing process. Each day, every moment would bear the burden of the past and open the way to the future for those who could see it as unique, unprecedented, and unrepeatable. Those who sought to react to the present in terms of the past would miss the moment. Those who refused to see the past as being fulfilled and corrected in the present would fail to understand that they were indeed in a new situation, with someone who spoke with uncanny authority, and who could say, 'Moses said unto you, but now I say unto.' Those who refused to see the future as beginning in the present would also miss the moment, while they returned to pay their respects to the dead, to tend their farms, or to celebrate the return of a lost son and brother.

Of course, the first Gospel began to be written in the midst of the civil war that consumed much of Palestine and razed Jerusalem from 66 to 73 CE. It was a time when anything could happen anywhere at any time. Terror and mercy, cruelty and devotion, lost their moorings in time and space. In Jerusalem during this time, days of ritual observance were disrupted by violence and rebellion; pleas for bread or mercy came from moment to moment; calls to surrender mixed with shouts of defiance: all of these occurring without any orchestration by priests or officials. There was no sacred or official calendar for suffering and defeat, victory or commemoration. Writing in the midst and in the aftermath of that holocaust, Gospel writers may well have had additional reason therefore to remember Jesus as someone who could live in the midst of chaos, in and for the moment, and thus respond with unfettered will and compassion to the immediacy of humans in need. It is not surprising that during these shattering times he was remembered as healing the sick or as feeding his disciples when the need arose rather than when the sacred calendar permitted. The Sabbath was made for man, he was recalled as having said: not man for the Sabbath. It is therefore also not surprising that the Gospel writers portrayed Jesus as someone who came in the nick of time: never too late to heal a sick child or even to revive a dead brother.

When anything can happen anywhere at any time, there is no wall – and no symbolic marker like sacred days and places – that can protect individuals from the terror of death. The only way to fight ubiquitous terror is to employ an equally ubiquitous source of healing and restoration. The only defense against imminent fatality would be an immanent source of life itself. The hero who is capable of withstanding cataclysm must be one whose gifts and presence require no particular location in time or space, and whose responses are immediate. This freedom, of course, brought him and his followers into close contact with gentiles, and in the early Church the boundaries between Jew and gentile became highly ambiguous, openly contested, and subjected to constant revision.

It is therefore not surprising that the Gospel writers portrayed Jesus as one who could live in the present as though it contained every possibility for good and evil. For them, the only way to enter into the present was with the radical freedom and self-determination that allowed Jesus to heal on the Sabbath, to tell others to let the dead bury the dead, and to turn his own face toward certain death in Jerusalem. In their accounts of Jesus, he displays no need for a mediator, and he addresses God the Father with unparalleled directness and immediacy, as if the apocalypse were indeed occurring in their midst.

Certainly, the Gospel narratives are edited with a view to heightening the contrast between Jesus, who is able to take the test of time, and his followers, who are unprepared for such an ordeal. The insistence of Jesus on meeting the needs of people without delay in the present is contrasted with the tendency of disciples to delay those who are seeking his immediate attention. The Gospel writers also contrast the ability of Jesus to take the test of time, to face his own death, with the disciples' inability to understand his words as referring to his coming crucifixion. Similarly, it is Jesus who rises to the occasion by staying alert throughout the night before his death on the cross, whereas the disciples sleep through the night and, with one possible exception, fail to stay with him as he is dying. Earlier it is Jesus who is willing to head toward certain death at Jerusalem, whereas it is the disciples who are portrayed as being unprepared for this final examination. They are unprepared for the graduation, the final departure, which is death.

Perhaps the civil war also heightened the tendency of the Gospel writers to draw heavily on the notion of the contest, the Greek *agon*, in which two forces are pitted against each other, only one of which will be able in the end to prevail. The contest begins with the temptation of Jesus, in which Satan seeks to divert him from his mission and to make him seek power that Satan himself has to offer. The Synoptic Gospels refer to Jesus' enemies as the legions of Satan or the demonic powers of the universe. Thus the apocalypse appears as an ongoing struggle in actual time, in the midst of the present, between the forces of good and evil arrayed against one another throughout the course of Jesus' life and ministry. Thus in his presence untold agony is given voice, when the demons cry out against him. Jesus encourages people with longstanding grievances to insist on immediate justice, and those with chronic maladies find in his presence the courage to ask for immediate healing. The secrets of an individual's past may be revealed, as in his conversations with a Samaritan woman who prefers to discuss differences in Judean and Samaritan religious traditions than to acknowledge her own previous alliances with several men. Note that these actors no longer need to be represented on a stage or to have their agony articulated for them through the voices of spirits. Their own time has come, to give their own testimony, and if they fail to do so, they have not understood their situation to be unique, unprecedented, and unrepeatable, and fateful for their future.

During that disastrous civil war, some of those who came to the city of Jerusalem, ostensibly to observe a ritual, came instead to settle old scores, assassinate old enemies, or destroy the records of debt kept at the treasury. Pilgrims coming for a feast day did not know whether an approaching stranger were a potential friend or carried a dagger under his cloak and concealed hostile intent. Anything could happen anywhere, at any time. In retrospect, Jesus' words about keeping lamps burning and being prepared at all times for a significant advent of some sort may have made even more sense to people shocked by the experience of seeing their holy city in flames and the streets choked with the bodies of the dead.

Under these conditions, it is not surprising that the Gospel writers were particularly sensitive to apocalyptic visions and imagery. Indeed, there is a heavy overlay in the Gospels of apocalyptic prediction, some of which is attributed to Jesus himself, in sayings retrospectively interpreted as referring to the civil war and the destruction of Jerusalem. It is all the more important to remember, therefore, that in the time of Jesus not everyone was caught up in apocalyptic enthusiasm and expectation. To be sure, some groups, notably those clustered under the name of Zealot, did harbor eschatological expectations of a Day on which the Kingdom of God would be initiated, but these were not necessarily widespread or normative for the population as a whole. On the other hand, well before the fall of Jerusalem in 66–73 CE, the polemical use of references to demons and Satan himself were the stock-in-trade of cultural warfare. It is all too easy to assimilate the pre-civil war of rhetoric of an *agon* between good and evil, God and Satan, to the apocalyptic imagery that enjoyed renewed currency in the aftermath of the civil war.

No doubt Jesus' enemies did accuse him of serving the arch-demon Beelzebub, especially if his contacts with people regarded as impure or alien were arousing suspicions of his conformity to the purity codes by which Israel maintained its sense of cultural distinctiveness. However, observance of the Torah was widely believed to provide an antidote to the Day of Judgment; so long as the Torah was studied and its laws observed, Israel would not run out of time. Indeed, Jesus is reported to have discouraged speculation among his disciples about the time and place of the coming of the Kingdom of God, while encouraging a radical form of obedience that would fulfill the law in unprecedented ways.

In this light, it becomes plausible to suggest that the apocalyptic framework within which the disciples may have experienced and understood their relationship to Jesus may have shifted over time. For instance, at least thirty years after Jesus' death, the destruction of Jerusalem seemed to fulfill a number of apocalyptic expectations, including some that could be attributed to Jesus himself. It is therefore inevitable that some scribal communities would have revised earlier accounts of Jesus and his ministry to include predictions of that later cataclysm and to define the Christian community as the sequel to the Temple itself.

Of course, it would be far too complex a task here to review the literature in which scholars have sought to identify the various layers of apocalyptic understanding that shaped the original experience of the disciples, their subsequent reflections on the death of Jesus, and the later impact of the civil war on the construction and editing of the Synoptic Gospels themselves. What is clear, however, is that the ideal of standing the test of time permeates both the Jewish and Hellenistic world in which the Christian community found its earliest roots. It is an ideal that is embedded in certain rites, in the classical Greek theater, and in the court. It is also an ideal deeply rooted in the Greek tradition of the *agon*.

Certainly, the notion of the *agon* permeates apocalyptic literature and popular expectations of a time not only when all tears will at last be wiped away but also of a critical test, for which many, if not all, will be sadly unprepared. It is a test in which some unexamined aspect of the past is brought to light, and in that moment all must answer for it or suffer what the Revelation of John the Divine (2:11) calls 'the second death' of being cast into eternal torment.

The Greek *agon* may well have been assimilated to Mesopotamian notions of a Last Judgment, originally perhaps Zoroastrian but eventually endemic within popular as well as scribal religiosity wherever Jews, Greeks, and Persians had mingled during and after the Exile. It underlies many of the warnings in the Revelation of John to the seven churches, that they will face a terrible judgment on the last day. One church does not love as it used to. Another church is following the ancient teaching of Balaam on food offered to idols, while still another church harbors a woman who has been given time to repent but who refuses to change her illicit ways. Still another church is failing to adhere to the teachings it received when it began, and so on. For each the message is that they are relinquishing or clinging to some aspect of their past, for which they will be judged, and that they are failing, despite their zeal, in the long contest with evil.

It is therefore not surprising that the notion of an apocalypse that is in the midst of people in their everyday life, which I have traced to the earlier days of the Jesus movement, would have been assimilated to these more generic Hellenistic and Mesopotamian apocalyptic scenarios, especially during and after the destruction of Jerusalem in the civil war, with their promises of a time yet to come, in which all sorrows will be assuaged, untold agony given a final voice, accounts settled at last, and a future of continuing ecstasy.

Furthermore, in the early Church there were regressive tendencies. Some factions were insisting that the new Christians, whether Jewish or gentile, be subject to all the laws of Israel: laws that insisted on circumcision for all converts and sought to control the way people would eat, relate to non-Jews, and observe holy days. Just as Pharisees had accused the followers of Jesus of laxity in these matters, so the Judaizers were seeking to deprive the early Church of its new freedom in the Gospel. The issue for many congregations was whether the traditionalists or the modernists were the true Jews, just as today the issue is whether the Christian right or the so-called mainstream denominations are the true Christians.

For some in the early Church there was no doubt on this matter: the test of time had already come. They no longer needed to hold on to the old view of history as heading toward a final confrontation between good and evil at some point in the future: an Armageddon, a final Day of Judgment, when the angels would take on the demons, and good would triumph once and for all over evil, with the sinners being consigned to eternal torment and the saved enjoying the unimpeded prospect of their own beatitude. That was because, in the life, death, and resurrection of Jesus, the final judgment had already begun, and henceforth everyone, Christians and non-Christians alike, were going to work out their own salvation in a mixture of freedom and holy fear. As the biblical scholar Peder Borgen puts it, for the earliest Christian community 'the new eschatological era had dawned.'[1]

In the early days it was not clear who were the true Jews (and who therefore were the real Christians): those who adhered to all the requirements, pertaining to diet, circumcision, and sacrifices, or those who took a more relaxed attitude toward these observances. Among the latter group were Jewish-Christians, whose association with gentile Christians required them to find a basis for their unity not in cultic practices but in the death of Jesus, which was taken to be the beginning of the new era in which Jews and gentiles now could live as one people (Borgen 1996: 287). Therefore, in the Revelation of John, the use of phrases like the 'synagogue of Satan' (Revelation 2:9, 3:9) to refer to certain Jews was an in-house controversy between Jews and Jewish Christians long before it become a classical site for locating Christian anti-Semitism (Borgen 1996: 285ff.). Indeed, even when, in the latter half of the fourth century, John Chrysostom of Antioch and the Council of Laodicea sought to draw sharp lines distinguishing Jews from Christians, the symbolic boundaries had become important precisely because, in actual fact, there was a great deal of socializing and interaction among Jews and Christians (Borden 1996: 289). That is when anti-Semitism becomes particularly useful: at times when it is hard to tell the difference between Jews and their detractors.

No doubt these later conflicts between Jewish and gentile Christians, on the one hand, and the more traditionalist Jews on the other, account in part for the prominent role played in the Synoptics by Jesus' controversies with the Pharisees. Uniformly the Pharisees are portrayed very much as the later 'Judaizers': hell-bent on fitting people for heaven by making them conform to a variety of observances during their lifetimes. These observances, so far as the Pharisees were concerned, were fasting and dieting, prayer on the Sabbath and cleanliness, along with the proper interpretation of Scripture. The Pharisees were therefore portrayed as ignoring the compulsions to openness and compassion that alone could be the basis for a new human community.

Although there is scholarly dispute on just how popular and influential were the Pharisees during Jesus' lifetime, there is some evidence that they still dominated popular conceptions of apocalyptic hope.[2] These conceptions focus on a heavenly reward for religious observance, and the Pharisees indeed believed in the immortality of the soul or in a resurrection after death to a much deserved fate in the next world (Powys 1997: 215). For some, that fate would be worse than death, whereas for others, on the last day, it would be a form of rebirth into lives that would be as good as they were enviable.

Needless to say, such an apocalyptic vision would have little appeal to a number of Palestinian Jews: least of all perhaps, to those who expected divine rule to be initiated through armed struggle, or to those, such as Qumran, who anticipated that their community would be the site of the new Israel, whereas the Temple and its corrupt elite would be destroyed. Pharisaic beliefs and practices were largely individual in focus rather than collective in scope, and they regarded the afterlife more as a consequence of one's good deeds in this world than a reward for which one could depend only on the mercy of God (Powys 1997: 218). The Pharisees offered little hope to those who could not afford the time or the money for such observances, and whose lives deprived them of a chance to achieve such purity, that is, to those who were primarily attracted to the movement of Jesus.

Just as the writers of the Synoptic Gospels characterized the Pharisees as part of the satanic legions seeking to throw impediments in the way of the Gospel and to deprive the people of God of their one true hope, so did the early churches stigmatize their traditionalist rivals as servants of Satan. Their traditionalist rivals claimed that they alone were the true Jews: those who adhered to all the requirements, pertaining to diet, circumcision, and sacrifices. Others also, however, claimed the mantle of Israel, and they took a more relaxed attitude toward those observances. However, their *agon* had already been fulfilled and decided in the life, death, and resurrection of Jesus. There was no need to wait for the outcome. Among this group were Jewish-Christians whose association with gentile Christians was requiring them to find a basis for their unity not in cultic practices but in the death of Jesus, which was taken to be the beginning of the new era in which Jews and gentiles at last could live as one people (Borgen 1996: 287).

However, some will still claim that to take apocalyptic beliefs out of the Christian canon would be to gut the Christian tradition of its essence. Certainly, apocalyptic rhetoric was the common coin of early religious polemic. Rome succeeded Babylon as the preferred object of eschatological hatred. As I have just noted with regard to early Christian polemics, the traditionalists, the Judaizers and the Pharisees took on the character of satanic forces arrayed against the people of God. More extreme groups were still waiting for the intervention of God in history in the form of a Teacher of Righteousness (Qumran) or seeking to precipitate that intervention through insurrection (the Zealots). These groups, too, also used the language of apocalypticism to defend their own expectations and to vilify their opponents as waging a losing battle on a cosmic scale. The Christian right's use of apocalyptic beliefs to consign other Christians to a world that is already passing away, along with that of the secular humanists, Muslims, and homosexuals has long-standing precedent in these first-century polemics.

Certainly, the folk religion of that time, throughout the Eastern Mediterranean, was filled with references to demons and angels, and many saw their illnesses and afflictions as being of demonic origin, just as they turned to angelic sources for their cure and salvation. Thus the apocalyptic imagination took the form of a wide range of beliefs: some in individual forms of triumph over the passage of time, others in collective victories at the end of history; some in a sudden break in the flow of time, others in an eventual consummation that would reward the long-suffering and faithful; some in an end of time that is the net result of a lifetime either of good or ill deeds, others in an end which comes about solely at the initiative of God. Indeed, some, like Paul, believed in an imminent end of time that would radically transform the situation of the dead as well as of the living, whereas others, also like Paul, believed that, for the sake of the missionary advance of the Gospel westward, it would be well to prepare for a much longer haul. Given this luxurious network of apocalyptic branches, to relieve the Christian community of its more vicious and vindictive, exclusively triumphalist apocalypticism would entail some careful but radical pruning: not the uprooting of the Christian faith itself.

I am arguing, however, that the pruning needs to be done. The Christian faith requires one to live as though the apocalypse were a present and continuing fact of life. The present is thus the time to settle old differences, give voice to untold agony, and to put the past where it belongs, so that the future can at last begin. Surely Borgen is right in saying that the early Christian community understood itself to be living in the midst of the Eschaton. The Last Things were going on all the time. In this belief, I would argue, they were remaining true to what the Synoptics reveal to have been at the heart of Jesus' ministry and message.

To begin with, of course, Jesus himself is known to have discouraged apocalyptic speculation. When he told his disciples not to say 'Lo here' or 'Lo there,' when anticipating the Kingdom, he was reminding them that the Kingdom could and would come anywhere, at any time, but to be sure of its place and timing was antithetical to its coming. That is because the Kingdom is in the midst of those who live with a requisite amount of intensity and expectation: not in some other time or place. Certainly, the future did not belong to those who, like some of his disciples, were spending their time wondering which one of them would be foremost in the coming Kingdom.

More than his injunctions against apocalyptic speculation suggest that the heart of Jesus' message had to do with his immediate presence among his followers. By reporting his legendary conversations with Martha and Mary, the Gospel writers reminded the Christian community that they have all the time in the world so long as they are with him and he with them. Thus it did not matter that he was not there when Lazarus died; in Jesus' presence there is time enough. It did matter, however, that while he was talking to Mary, Martha was missing the moment, preoccupied as she was with things that simply had to be done.

That every moment is potentially as crucial as the cross itself is the burden of one story in the Synoptic Gospels after another. The Good Samaritan is good because he recognizes and responds to the needs of the moment, and he attends to the fallen traveler, whereas the priests and Levites are preoccupied by their need to be somewhere else at another time. The familiar parable of the prodigal son makes the same point: that the long-standing obedience of the elder brother to his father should not stand in the way of the father's response to the uniqueness of the moment in which his son, long thought to be lost, is suddenly found. Over and over again, the Gospel stories make the same injunction: hire the laborers at the eleventh hour and pay them a full day's wage; it is not chronology that counts but the needs of the moment. Let the people along the roadside get to Jesus; although the disciples typically seek to forestall them, Jesus engages in an immediate response. The needy do not have to wait, and they do not need the mediation of the disciples to get to Jesus.

This radical claim to immediacy is at the root of the stories and parables that put such a high premium on the swift satisfaction of human need. Think of the parables about lost sheep, lost coins, buried treasures. In every story the point is the same: drop everything else and go after what has been lost. Consider also the many parables about the coming of the Kingdom. Whether the coming King is compared with a returning, formerly absentee landowner or to a bridegroom does not matter. What does matter is that no one should be found unable to rise to that occasion. Keep the lamps lighted for the bridegroom. Settle all your outstanding accounts quickly. Do not take 'No' for an answer from the judge but pressure him relentlessly until he meets your family's needs. Whether it is stories about letting the sick and the hungry get to Jesus, or parables about the coming of a Kingdom, the Gospels have no truck with delay and mediation.

None of these accounts portrays Jesus as keeping people waiting because he is standing on ceremony. In contrast to those who are worried about purity, he allows the impure, whether they were menstruating women or the sick and the dying, to get to him. Regardless of injunctions about the need to observe the Sabbath, he heals the sick and feeds his disciples on that day. The Sabbath is, after all, made for man: not man for the Sabbath. There is no room in the Gospels for elevating Jesus to a higher order of being. Thus he disclaims any magical powers by which he has healed people. It is the people's own faith that has healed them: not his own charisma. They do not need a mediator.

How, given the overwhelming consistency of these teachings, parables, and stories, could the early Christian community ever understand itself other than as being in the midst of the apocalypse? Every moment is potentially unique and unprecedented. That is why the community remembered stories in which Jesus told people not to miss the moment in which their souls are required of them: the moment when someone is in jail and needs a visitor, or is hungry and needs to be fed, or is naked and needs to be clothed. That is the moment that separates the sheep from the goats: not some day long in the future but in the present, whenever someone responds to human need without a theological reason for doing so. Any moment may be unprecedented and unique; that is why the community remembered stories in which Jesus told people to leave their unburied relatives behind, if that were necessary in order to follow Him. His was not a general injunction to establish a principle of non-burial, but a command to ignore sacred precedent when it stands in the way of the unique and unprecedented.

No moment is definitely and obviously momentous. That is why the community remembered injunctions against defining some times and places as sacred at the expense of others. Thus Jesus refuses to go on pilgrimage to the Temple until his time has come, and as for the Temple of the future, it will not be made by hands but will be the result of the Spirit coming, whenever, wherever, and to whomever it will. Every moment may be the time in which the secrets of the past are revealed, but no particular moment is certain to be momentous. That is why the community remembered stories like that in which Jesus conversed with the Samaritan woman at the well. She wanted to have a religious discussion about the traditions honored by Judeans and Samaritans, who preferred different mountaintops for their rites, whereas Jesus reminded her that the relevant past was the one she was refusing to discuss: her marriages to five different men over time. As in any apocalyptic moment, the secrets of the heart would then be shouted from the housetops.

In the light of such immediate revelation, it was not tradition and lineage that mattered; God could raise children of Abraham out of the very stones of the street. What did matter was the ability of two or three, when they gathered together, to invoke his presence. His spirit would come, and when it did, the future would always begin. To engage in such an encounter, however, individuals would have to graduate from their past and enter into a moment that was unrepeatable and irreversible in its consequences. Those who looked back prove themselves unable to stand the test of time. They would require liturgies that permit repetition and thus extend the critical moment over time.

The Gospels are full of reminders that the disciples did not understand what Jesus was saying about his death, and when he was with them in the Garden of Gethsemane the night before his death, it was his disciples, again, who did not understand how unique, unprecedented, and irreversible was that time. They slept while he watched. Again at his trial, and yet again during his crucifixion, the disciples were notable by their absence; they missed the moment. Even the encounters with the risen Christ are marked by delayed recognition, and in the earliest account it is entirely clear that once again the disciples are running late; Jesus has gone on ahead of them into Galilee. Thus the disciples serve the symbolic function of portraying the opposite of the Gospel's message: a reminder to later audiences about what it means fully to be present in time.

That is, the Gospels spell out what it meant for the earliest Church to live as though the future had begin: to live 'apocalyptically,' for lack of a better word. The experience of the early Church continued to influence what certain stories, sayings, and parables would mean to them over time, so that they may actually have felt as if they had not understood them fully the first time around. Thus their own experience, as they found that the past was becoming clear, as old burdens were being released, and as suppressed agony and animosity were indeed coming to the surface, indicated to them that they were indeed in a new situation. The future had been beginning for some time.

It also became clear, however, how difficult it is to graduate from the past: how easy it would be to slip back into following the old requirements for cleanliness, sacrifice, diet, and observance that had been imposed on them by the Pharisees and that continued to be touted by the 'Judaizers' and traditionalists. If they used the rhetoric of demons and Satan to describe their encounters with their enemies, they did so in the understanding that they were living in the midst of an ongoing and continuous apocalypse: not in anticipation of some Day of Judgment yet to come.

Thus the Gospel narratives themselves reflect a new situation in which the visions of the traditional scribal communities, already quite many and diverse, were increasingly contested, and the faithful were not confined to a particular community's canons of interpretation.[3] Jesus had not taught as the scribes but had possessed an authority of his own that was unique and unprecedented. Even more the point, the Galilean world in which he was preaching, teaching, and healing was little concerned with apocalyptic scenarios that envisaged the destruction of the Jerusalem Temple with its corrupt priesthood. Although some have claimed that there was a Galilean apocalyptic tradition that shows up in documents, such as 1 Enoch, there is reasonably reliable evidence that the Galileans willingly maintained their connection with the Jerusalem Temple through tithes and pilgrimages as a way of claiming their own continuing inheritance of the land (Freyne 1988: 190). On the other hand, some of the people of Galilee had little enthusiasm for coming to the defense of the Jerusalem Temple in the civil war of 66–73 CE, not because they were pro-Roman so much as because they were neutral or even pacifist (Freyne 1988: 190). It is not surprising, therefore, that in the Synoptic Gospels there is not the tendency to demonize Rome as another Babylon that there is in the Revelation of John.

If, in the editorial composition of the Gospel stories, an apocalyptic framework is imposed on the stories, sayings, and parables of Jesus, it comes from the scribal communities that compiled the Gospels in the aftermath of the devastating civil war of 66–73 CE and the destruction of Jerusalem and its Temple. The more traditional framework that looked forward to a Day of Judgment with compensatory disasters to be inflicted on a wide range of oppressors conflicts with the idea that every day is filled with apocalyptic significance simply because the moment itself may well be unprecedented, potentially revelatory of past sufferings, decisive for the relation of the individual to the past and the future, and therefore irreversible in its consequences. In such moments, individuals live through the revelation that is integral to the apocalyptic vision: the discovery of a past that they had failed or refused to recognize, and of a future that they may have gone to great lengths to avoid. Thus the disciples complain that they have left everything to follow Jesus, only to discover that he offers them no security, no resting-place, and possible execution. If the disciples are portrayed as being surprised by this discovery, it is because they figure in the Gospel narratives as individuals who were perennially oblivious to the apocalyptic significance of the moments in which they were engaged: unprepared to find that their history pointed toward the crucifixion of their leader and that their leader in turn would offer them a future not of apocalyptic triumph but of continuing and radical uncertainty.

Stories of the disciples' alleged inability to understand the presence of Jesus are intended to throw the hearer or reader into an unprecedented situation that will cast the past and the future in a new light, just as the Jesus movement itself introduces a future for which most were unprepared and for which many may have had very little enthusiasm: a future that brings rejection and death long before it provides them with the tokens of triumph. *The telling of the Gospel itself is intended to perform the apocalypse.*

The Christian right does not share this understanding of the apocalypse, since they adhere to the version that postpones the apocalypse to the end of a history culminating in the final, cataclysmic events foretold in the Revelation of John and interpolated in the Gospels in certain passages such as Matthew 24–25. Their attempts to make the present part of the apocalypse still are based on an imaginary universe in which there are only two kinds of people: the sons of Abraham and the peoples of Babylon: people we have now discovered who include secular humanists and homosexuals as well as New Age religionists and Muslims. Pat Robertson and his followers, along with the mass audiences of the Christian right, still do not understand the apocalyptic aspects of everyday life in the way that the Synoptic Gospels, at least, disclose them.

Granted that even in these Gospels there are passages that reflect the apocalyptic imagination of the writer of the Revelation of John, the Synoptics are quite clear that the disciples and the early Christian community are living in the thick of an apocalyptic world. The past kept changing and catching up with them, just as their present continued to give the past new meaning. They were literally on their own in a new situation, not only because traditional authorities were of little use in a world with so many and various scribal traditions and apocalyptic visions, but because the civil war and the sacking of Jerusalem had plunged them into a truly unprecedented situation and could never be reversed. In that world, the emphasis of the Jesus movement on living as though the past and the future were imploding into the present and that one's every word or deed might prove revelatory or fateful made new sense, and the telling of the Gospel stories themselves was intended to place new audiences in precisely that same situation of radical openness to the past and the future.

It is no doubt easier to think of the apocalypse as lying in a future that could erupt within their lifetimes, but which might be indefinitely delayed, rather than to think of every moment as unprecedented, potentially revelatory, and irreversible in its consequences. Thus many simply did not – and still do not – understand the role of the Jesus movement in secularizing the apocalypse by making it a part of the mundane world rather than postponing it to a mysterious time and place. It is not easy or natural to live into the continuing apocalypse of everyday life, to apprehend the uniqueness and unprecedented character of the moment, to come to terms with a past that is never what it used to be, and to enter a future for which one is chronically unprepared. Therefore many, like the disciples and the 'Judaizers,' and like the scribal communities that added to the Gospels some of their own highly conventional visions of the apocalypse, still imagined that there would be yet another day on which they could hope to pass the test of time. Many others no doubt settled for the routine household codes and guides for ethical living that appear in the epistles rather than seeking to understand what might be potentially at stake in the moment. To spread out the apocalypse over time has long been, and still remains, the first line of defense against taking the test of time. No wonder, then, that for the Christian right the apocalypse still lies at some point in the future and that it will be accompanied by the most horrific catastrophes, for which only they will be spared. They may be right about the catastrophes, but if they are, it may be in part because the Protestant and Catholic churches have failed to realize that they have provided theological support for the failure of the nation as a whole to understand, take responsibility for, and complete its past and to allow a future to begin that will not recycle ancient hatreds into new cataclysms.

Notes

1   Peder Borgen, *Early Christianity and Hellenistic Judaism*. Edinburgh: T&T Clark, 1996, p. 290.
2   David Powys, *'Hell': A Hard Look at a Hard Question. The Fate of the Unrighteous in New Testament Thought*. Carlisle, Cumbria: Paternoster Press, 1997, p. 213.
3   Sean Freyne, *Galilee, Jesus, and the Gospels: Literary Approaches and Historical Investigations*. Philadelphia: Fortress Press, 1988, p. 43.

Bibliography

Alexander, Paul J., *The Byzantine Apocalyptic Tradition*, Berkeley and Los Angeles: University of California Press, 1985.

Altizer, Thomas J.J., 'Modern Thought and Apocalypticism,' in *The Encyclopedia of Apocalypticism*, Vol. 3, *Apocalypticism in the Modern Period and the Contemporary Age*, edited by Stephen J. Stein, New York: Continuum Publishing, 2000: 325–59.

Amanat, Abbas, 'The Resurgence of Apocalyptic in Modern Islam,' in *The Encyclopedia of Apocalypticism*, Vol. 3, *Apocalypticism in the Modern Period and the Contemporary Age*, edited by Stephen J. Stein, New York: Continuum Publishing, 2000: 230–64.

Asad, Talal, *Formations of the Secular: Christianity, Islam, and Modernity*, Stanford, California: Stanford University Press, 2003.

Ayoub, Mahmoud, *Redemptive Suffering in Islam*, The Hague, Paris, and New York: Mouton Publishers, 1978.

Baillie, Gil, *Violence Unveiled: Humanity at the Crossroads*, New York: Crossroad Press, 1995.

Barr, David L., 'Waiting for the End that Never Comes: The Narrative Logic of John's Story,' in *Studies in the Book of Revelation*, edited by Steve Moyise, Edinburgh and New York: T&T Clark, 2001: 101–112.

Berlet, Chip and Matthew N. Lyons, *Right-Wing Populism in America: Too Close for Comfort*, New York and London: The Guilford Press, 2000.

Bollas, Christopher, *On Being a Character*, London: Routledge, 2003.

Boxall, Ian, 'The Many Faces of Babylon the Great: *Wirkunggescghicte* and the Interpretation of Revelation 17' in *Studies in the Book of Revelation* edited by Steven Moyise, Edinburgh and New York: T&T Clark, 2001.

Caciola, Nancy, 'Spirits seeking bodies: death, Possession and Communal Memory in the Middle Ages,' in *The Place of the Dead. Death and Remembrance in Late Medieval and Early Modern Europe*, edited by Bruce Gordon and Peter Marshall, Cambridge: Cambridge University Press, 2000: 66–86.

Cancik, Hubert, 'The End of the World, of History, and of the Individual in Greek and Roman Antiquity,' in *The Encyclopedia of Apocalypticism*, Vol. 1, *The Origins of Apocalypticism in Judaism and*

Christianity, edited by John J. Collins, New York and London: Continuum Press, 2000: 84–125.

Chapman, Mark D., 'The Coming Crisis. The Impact of Eschatology on Theology in Edwardian England,' in *Journal for the Study of the New Testament*, Supplement Series 208, edited by Stanley E. Porter, Sheffield: Sheffield Academic Press, 2001.

Clifford, Richard J., 'The Roots of Apocalypticism in Near Eastern Myth,' in *The Encyclopedia of Apocalypticism*, Vol. 1, *The Origins of Apocalypticism in Judaism and Christianity*, edited by John J. Collins, New York and London: Continuum Press, 2000: 3–38.

Cohn, Norman, *Cosmos, Chaos, and the World to Come: The Ancient Roots of Apocalyptic Faith*, second edition, New Haven and London: Yale University Press, 2001.

Collins, Adela Yarbro, 'The Book of Revelation,' in *The Encyclopedia of Apocalypticism*. Vol. 1. *The Origins of Apocalypticism in Judaism and Christianity*, edited by John J. Collins, New York and London: Continuum, 2000: 384–414.

Collins, John J., 'Introduction to Book 4,' in *The Old Testament Pseudepigrapha*, Vol. 1, *Apocalyptic Literature and Testaments*, edited by James H. Charlesworth, New York: Doubleday, 1983.

Collins, John J., *The Apocalyptic Imagination: An Introduction to the Jewish Matrix of Christianity*, New York: Crossroad, 1987.

Collins, John J., editor, *The Encyclopedia of Apocalypticism*, Vol. I, *The Origins of Apocalypticism in Judaism and Christianity*, New York, London: Continuum, 2000.

Cyril of Jerusalem, 'Lecture 5: The Eucharist, in *Prayers of the Eucharist: Early and Reformed*, edited by R.C.D. Jasper and G.J. Cuming, London: Collins Publishers, 1975: 53.

Denzey, Nicola, 'The Limits of Ethnic Categories,' in *Handbook of Early Christianity: Social Science Approaches*, edited by Anthony Blasé, Jean Duhaime, and Paul-Andre Durcotte, Walnut Creek, CA: Altamira Press, 2002.

Donne, John, 'Divine Meditations 13, ll. 1–4,' in *The Complete English Poems*, edited by A.J. Smith, revised edition, London: 1986.

Donne, John, *Suicide*, transcribed and edited by William A. Clebsch, Chico, California: Scholars Press, Studies in the Humanities Series No. 1, 1983.

Ellison, Christopher and Darren E. Sherkat, 'Conservative Protestantism and Support for Corporal Punishment,' in *American Sociological Review*, 1993, Vol. 58, (February): 131–44.

Ezekiel the Tragedian, *Exagoge* l. 147–8, translated and introduced by R.G. Robertson, in *The Old Testament Pseudepigrapha*, Vol. 1, edited by James H. Charlesworth, Garden City, New York: Doubleday, 1983.

Foard, James H., 'Imagining Nuclear Weapons: Hiroshima, Armageddon, and the Annihilation of the Students of Ichijo School,' in *Journal of the American Academy of Religion*, LXV/1, Spring, 1997: 1–18.

Gordon, Bruce, 'Malevolent Ghosts and Ministering Angels: Apparitions and Pastoral Care in the Swiss Reformation,' in *The Place of the Dead. Death and Remembrance in Late Medieval and Early Modern Europe*, edited by Bruce Gordon and Peter Marshall, Cambridge: Cambridge University Press, 2000: 87–109.

Gorenberg, Gershom, *The End of Days. Fundamentalism and the Struggle for the Temple Mount*, New York and London: Oxford University Press, 2000.

Halbwachs, Maurice, *On Collective Memory*, edited, translated, and with an introduction by Lewis A. Coser, Chicago and London: University of Chicago Press, 1992.

Isaac, E., I Enoch, 103, 6–8; 104, 3–5, in '1 (Ethiopic Apocalypse of) Enoch. (Second Century BC–First Century AD) A New Translation and Introduction by E. Isaac,' in *The Old Testament Pseudepigrapha*, Vol. 1, edited by James H. Charlesworth, Garden City, New York: Doubleday, 1983: 5–89.

Jasper, R.C.D. and G.J. Cuming, *Prayers of the Eucharist Early and Reformed*, London: Collins Publishers, 1975.

Kermode, Frank, *The Sense of an Ending: Studies in the Theory of Fiction with a New Epilogue*, New York and Oxford: Oxford University Press, 2000.

Kirk, G.S., Raven, J.E. and Schofield, M., eds., *The Presocratic Philosophers: A Critical History with a Selection of Texts*, Cambridge: Cambridge University Press, second edition, 1983.

Kristof, Nicholas D., 'Apocalypse Now?', *The New York Times*, Book Review Desk, December 12, 1999.

Lamy, Philip, 'Secularizing the Millennium: Survivalist, Militias, and the New World Order,' in *Millennium, Messiahs, and Mayhem. Contemporary Apocalyptic Movements*, edited by Thomas Robbins and Susan J. Palmer, New York and London: Routledge, 1997: 93–119.

LeDuff, Charlie, 'Threats and Responses: Deployment; As an American Armada leaves San Diego, Tears are the Rule of the Day.' *The New York Times*, Foreign Desk, January 18, 2003.

LeGoff, Jacques, *History and Memory*, translated by Steven Rendall and Elizabeth Claman, New York: Columbia University Press, 1992.

Lienesch, Michael, *Redeeming America: Piety and Politics in the New Christian Right*, Chapel Hill and London: University of North Carolina Press, 1993.

Lindsey, Hal with C.C. Carlson, *The Late Great Planet Earth*, Grand Rapids, Mich.: Zondervan Publishing, 1970.

Marshall, Peter '"The map of God's word": Geographies of the Afterlife in Tudor and Early Stuart England," in *The Place of the Dead. Death and Remembrance in Late Medieval and Early Modern Europe*, edited by Bruce Gordon and Peter Marshall, Cambridge: Cambridge University Press, 2000: 110–30.

Metzger, Bruce M. 'The Fourth Book of Ezra,' translated, edited, and with an introduction by B. M. Metzger, in *The Old Testament Pseudepigrapha*, Vol. 1, edited by James H. Charlesworth, Garden City, New York: Doubleday, 1983: 517–59.

Moaddel, Mansoor, 'Ideology as Episodic Discourse: The Case of the Iranian Revolution,' in *American Sociological Review*, Vol. 57, Issue 3 (June 1992): 353–79.

Moorhead, James H., *American Apocalypse: Yankee Protestants and the Civil War 1860–1869*, New Haven: Yale University Press, 1978.

Moorhead, James H., 'Apocalypticism in Mainstream Protestantism,' in *The Encyclopedia of Apocalypticism*, Vol. 3, *Apocalypticism in the Modern Period and the Contemporary Age*, edited by Stephen J. Stein, New York: Continuum Publishing, 2000.

Nabokov, Isabelle, *Religion Against the Self*, New York and London: Oxford University Press, 2000.

Office of Theology and Worship, *Between Millennia: What Presbyterians Believe About the Coming of Christ*, Louisville, KY: The Presbyterian Church (USA), 2001.

O'Keefe, Daniel Lawrence, *Stolen Lightning*, New York: Vintage Books, 1983.

O'Leary, Stephen D., 'Popular Culture and Apocalypticism,' in *The Encyclopedia of Apocalypticism*, Vol. 3, *Apocalypticism in the Modern Period and the Contemporary Age*, edited by Stephen J. Stein, New York: Continuum Publishing, 2000: 392–426.

Panourgia, Neni, *Fragments of Death, Fables of Identity: An Athenian Anthropography*, Madison, Wisconsin: University of Wisconsin Press, 1995.

Paul, Ian, 'The Book of Revelation: Image, Symbol, and Metaphor,' in *Studies in the Book of Revelation*, edited by Steve Moyise, Edinburgh and New York: T&T Clark, 2001: 131–48.

Pescosolido, Bernice A., and Sharon Georgianna, 'Durkheim, Suicide, and Religion: Toward a Network Theory of Suicide,' in *American Sociological Review*, Vol. 54, Issue 1 (February 1988): 33–48.

Priest, J., 'Testament of Moses: A New Translation and Introduction,' in *The Old Testament Pseudepigrapha*, Vol. 1, *Apocalyptic Literature and Testaments*, edited by James H. Charlesworth, New York: Doubleday, 1983: 919–34.

Qutb, Sayyid, *Islam and Universal Peace*, Plainfield, Indiana: American Trust Publications, 1993.

Qutb, Sayyid, 'Ma'alim fi al-Tariq,' quoted in Lawrence Wright, 'The Man Behind Bin Laden,' *The New Yorker*, September 16, 2002: 56–85.

Robertson, Pat, *The New World Order*, Dallas, London, Vancouver, Melbourne: Word Publishing, 1991.

Robertson, R.G., *Exagoge* l, 'Ezekiel the Tragedian,' translated and introduced by R. G. Robertson, in *The Old Testament Pseudepigrapha*, Vol. 1, edited by James H. Charlesworth, Garden City, New York: Doubleday, 1983.

Roth, Andrew L., '"Men Wearing Masks"' Issues of Description in the Analysis of Ritual,' in *Sociological Theory*, Vol. 13, Issue 3 (November 1995): 301–27.

Runciman, David, 'A Bear Armed with a Gun,' in *London Review of Books*, Vol. 25, Number 7, April 2003a: 3–6.

Runciman, David, 'The Politics of Good Intentions,' in *London Review of Books*, Vol. 25, Number 9, May 2003b: 3, 6–8, 12.

Schoepflin, Renni B., 'Apocalypticism in an Age of Science,' in *The Encyclopedia of Apocalypticism*, Vol. 3, *Apocalypticism in the Modern Period and the Contemporary Age*, edited by Stephen J. Stein, New York: Continuum Publishing, 2000: 427–41.

Schwartz, Barry, 'Memory as a Cultural System: Abraham Lincoln in World War II,' in *American Sociological Review*, Vol. 61, Issue 5 (October 1996): 908–27.

Smith, David Norman, 'The Social Construction of Enemies: Jews and the Representation of Evil,' in *Sociological Theory*, Vol. 14, Issue 3 (November 1996): 203–40.

Smith, Dennis C., *The Story of the Rescue Efforts at the World Trade Center*, New York: Viking, 2002.

Smith, Jane Idleman and Yvonne Yazbeck Haddad, *The Islamic Understanding of Death and Resurrection*, New York and London: Oxford University Press, 2000.

Smolinski, Reiner, 'Apocalypticism in Colonial North America,' in *The Encyclopedia of Apocalypticism*, Vol. 3, *Apocalypticism in the Modern Period and the Contemporary Age*, edited by Stephen J. Stein, New York: Continuum Publishing, 2000: 36–71.

Spencer, Jonathan, *A Sinhala Village in as Time of Trouble: Politics and Changes in Rural Sri Lanka*, Delhi: Oxford University Press, 1990.

Stowell, Daniel W., *Rebuilding Zion. The Religious Reconstruction of the South, 1863–1877*, New York and Oxford: Oxford University Press, 1998.

Virgil, *The Aeneid*, translated by Robert Fitzgerald, New York: Vintage Books, 1990.

Weber, Eugen, *Apocalypses. Prophecies, Cults, and Millennial Beliefs through the Ages*, Cambridge: Harvard University Press, 1999.

Wright, Lawrence, 'The Man Behind Bin Laden,' *The New Yorker*, September 16, 2002: 56–85.

Index